OTHER WAYS, OTHER MEANS:
Altered Awareness Activities for Receptive Learning

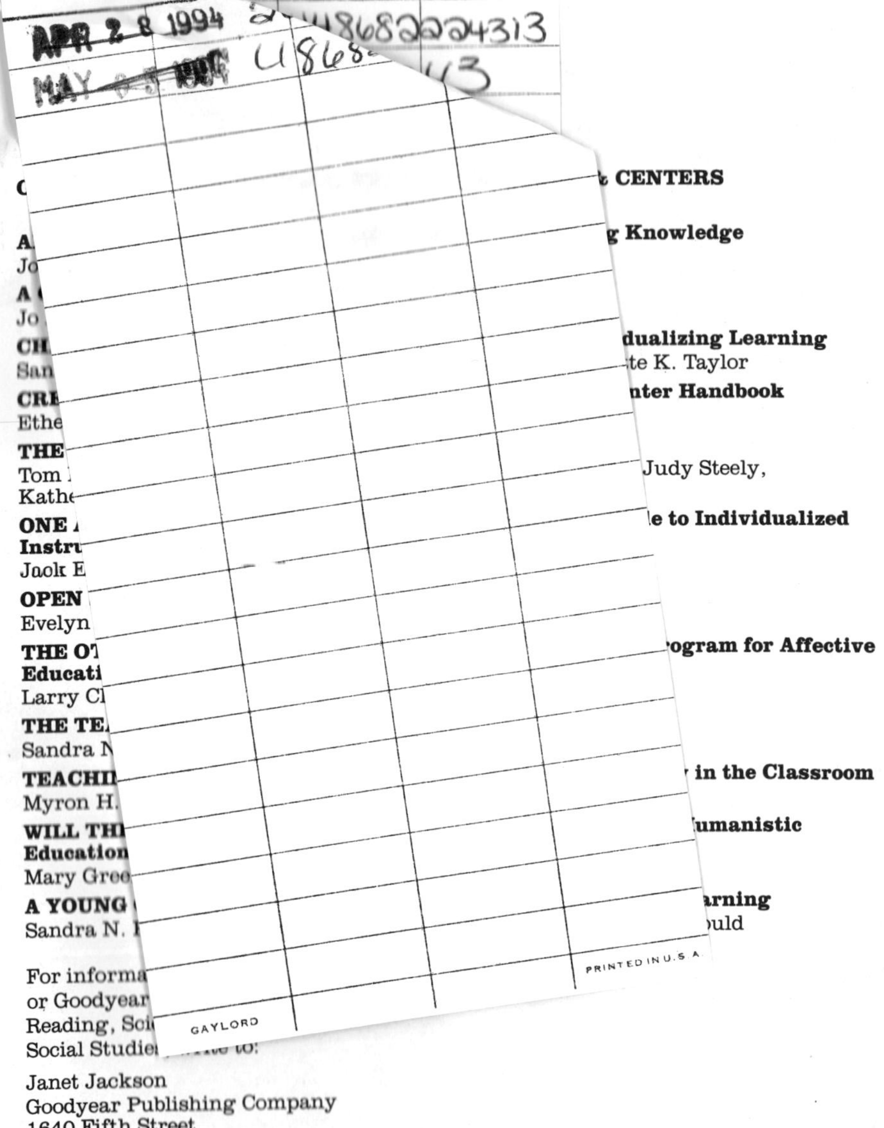

C… … CENTERS

A… …g Knowledge
Jo…

A … …
Jo…

CH… …dualizing Learning
San… …te K. Taylor

CRE… …nter Handbook
Ethe…

THE…
Tom … … Judy Steely,
Kathe…

ONE … …e to Individualized
Instru…
Jack E…

OPEN …
Evelyn…

THE OT… …ogram for Affective
Educati…
Larry Cl…

THE TE…
Sandra N…

TEACHI… …y in the Classroom
Myron H.…

WILL THI… …umanistic
Education…
Mary Gree…

A YOUNG … …arning
Sandra N. … …uld

For informa…
or Goodyear…
Reading, Sci…
Social Studie… …rite to:

Janet Jackson
Goodyear Publishing Company
1640 Fifth Street
Santa Monica, CA 90401
(213) 393-6731

OTHER WAYS, OTHER MEANS:

Altered Awareness Activities for Receptive Learning

Practical Teaching Strategies for the Use of: RELAXATION
IMAGERY
DREAMS
SUGGESTOLOGY-
HYPNOSIS
MEDITATION

Alton Harrison, Jr.
Diann Musial

NORTHERN ILLINOIS UNIVERSITY

GOODYEAR PUBLISHING COMPANY, INC.
SANTA MONICA, CALIFORNIA

Library of Congress Cataloging in Publication Data
Harrison, Alton.
Other ways, other means.
(Goodyear education series)
Includes bibliographies and index.
1. Learning, Psychology of.   2. Meditation.
3. Hypnotism.   4. Phychical research.   I. Musial,
Diann, joint author.   II. Title.
LB1053.H37   370.15'2   77-14045
ISBN 0-87620-629-1
ISBN 0-87620-628-3 pbk.

Y-6283-9 (paper)
Y-6291-2 (case)
Current Printing (last digit):
10 9 8 7 6 5 4 3 2 1

Interior & cover design: Kitty R. Anderson
Illustrations: Peg Reynolds
Art production: Emily J. Beebee

Printed in the United States of America

CONTENTS

ACKNOWLEDGEMENTS

The authors acknowledge
the contributions of
Barrie Jean Barrett,
Peg Reynolds,
Jean Anne McGrath
and Jill Stefani.

1111111 INTRODUCTION 11

The truth is that we are doomed, by the fact that we are practical beings with very limited tasks to attend to, and special ideals to look after, to be absolutely blind and insensible to the inner feelings, and to the whole inner significance of lives that are different from their own. Our opinion of the worth of such lives is absolutely wide of the mark, and unfit to be counted at all.

WILLIAM JAMES

Recent research has verified the fact that the right and left sides of the human brain perform different functions. The left cerebral hemisphere is specialized to perform rational, linear, and digital functions while the right cerebral hemisphere performs intuitive, metaphoric, and analogic functions. Thus, we have two cerebral approaches to the acquisition of knowledge and the discovery of truth. One is rational, linear, and logical. The other is intuitive, metaphoric, and capricious [**13, 19, 20**]. Transpersonal education is the use of altered states of consciousness to integrate these two learning modes.

Our highest creative achievements are the products of the complementary functioning of the two modes. Our intuitive knowledge is never explicit, never precise in the scientific sense. It is only when the intellect can begin to process the intuitive leaps, to explain and "translate" the intuition into operational and functional knowledge, that scientific understanding becomes complete. [**13, p. 12**]

Transpersonal education is based on the premise that the integration of physical, emotional, intellectual, and spiritual development in accordance with inner truth is of paramount importance in the life of every individual. The meaning and purpose of specific objects, events, and relationships in life are probed through subjective experiences as well as through scientific inquiry. Transpersonal education stresses affective or intrinsic learning through self-discovery and transcendence.

> If we look at how the most creative scientists such as Einstein actually describe their work, they report intuitive visualization, namely right-brain activity, comes first, followed by reasoning. Some scientists describe actually seeing the abstraction they think about. For example, Friedrich von Kekule discovered the benzene ring and other insights pertaining to organic chemistry using a creative visual reverie, a mild altered state of consciousness commonly described as a daydreaming state. [17, p. 15]

Such an approach to learning is in harmony with the philosophic construct of transcendentals. Truth, Beauty, and Goodness have puzzled epistemological thinkers throughout the ages. How does one define these universal realities? Is the label "universal" sufficient? Truth, Beauty, and Goodness not only belong to the particular and the whole but have an existence that supercedes and impregnates the totality of Being. It is this problem of superceding, of having a cosmic essence, that defies accurate philosophic explanation. Plato left the problem unsolved and merely delegated Beauty, Truth, and Goodness to the World of Ideas. Aristotle recognized the problem of their cosmic nature, as did Aquinas, but they also left the question unresolved. Perhaps humanity is ready once again to approach the problem of the transcendentals from a perspective of consciousness, or, more precisely, from an altered state of consciousness. Possibly, the problem of the transcendentals can only be discerned from within. If in fact it is human nature to participate in a cosmic existence, if in fact a human being is the individual self immersed in a cosmic reality, then transpersonal learning may be the most logical approach to the True, the Beautiful, and the Good.

The origins of transpersonal education can be traced to a fairly recent school of thought known as transpersonal psychology. The pioneers of this movement were convinced that many of our experiences suggested a reality that went beyond our present concepts of time and space. They envisioned a need for a psychology that would focus on the spiritual nature and the search for significance [15]. Transpersonal psychology tends to be more cosmic in scope than the behavioristic, psychoanalytic, and humanistic psychologies and offers a more inclusive vision of human potential. It has focused attention on altered states of consciousness, subjective experiences, and psychic phenomena, most of which have been either ignored or disdained by traditional psychology.

Dr. Thomas Roberts and Dr. Frances Clark have led the movement to translate and apply the principles and research findings of transpersonal psychology to the field of education. They define the optimal educational environment as one that stimulates and nurtures the intuitive as well as the rational, the imaginative as well as the practical, and the creative as well as the receptive functions of each individual [17]. The educational conceptualizing of both Roberts and Clark is heavily influenced by humanistic psychology in general and Maslow in particular. Clark has formulated a transpersonal extension of Maslow's theory. Clark contends that every human being carries within his or her own life the only real and possible standards by which to measure adjustment—the actualization of selfhood. She points out that individuals continually seek to integrate their lives in accordance with their own inner truth rather than in accordance with authoritarian doctrines or prescribed truth. Transpersonal education is an affirmation of these intuitively discovered, self-validated values. A basic assumption underlying transpersonal education is that each person must trust his or her biological nature in order to transcend the conscious ego and time and space as well [2].

Such dependence on the senses to transcend is often approached as a problem of the mind-body dichotomy. Plato [14] spoke of the body

as a dark shell that shadows us from union with the true World of Ideas. Aristotle refined such a view by looking at mind and body as a unit. All information about the particular was sensed by the body; the mind's abstractions of these particular sense impressions then generated universal constructs. Descartes and his followers formalized the mind-body problem into a dichotomy and, in a sense, returned to the Platonic system of mind being the ultimate: "I think, therefore I am" [3]. Kant returned to the Aristotelian framework and attempted to reunite body and mind. He held that knowledge or truth was the product of an individual's inductive sensory processing modes or categories. The content of ultimate truth came through sense impressions but its form was determined by the deductive mode of one's intellectual functions. Ultimate realities or truths, if existent, could be known only in a subjective fashion. Mind and body were one and their interactive, cognitive functioning was the basis for truth.

Kant's brilliant exposé of categorical reasoning [9] has remained a respected theory but has left philosophers dissatisfied. If man can know only in a certain categorical fashion, can truth as it really is ever be comprehended? Once again, it would seem that the question of knowing can be approached through transpersonal learning. Kant's problem of knowing only in a human way may not be a problem after all. If one accepts the assumption of the self participating in a cosmic existence beyond time and space, and if one accepts transpersonal learning as a mode of learning equal to and interrelated with categorical linear learning, then knowing in a human fashion is not limiting. The heart of the problem is just this assumption. One must accept intuition, ecstasy, and insight as valid modes of knowing. If this can be accepted, then Kant's limitations are not limitations at all. We can know in a categorical, linear fashion as well as a cosmic, nonlinear fashion. Reality, structured and unstructured, particular and universal, personal and cosmic, in all its seeming dichotomies, is harmonized in the human brain by its left and right cerebral knowing functions.

Historically, education has concentrated on the development of the rational or left-brain powers while virtually ignoring affective or right-brain development. Because of this, transpersonal educators tend to overemphasize the right-brain mode of learning. Therefore, at the risk of being radical, we emphasize that transpersonal education seeks a **balance** between the affective and cognitive rather than a **reversal** of the present cognitive imbalance. "Transpersonal psychology in education does not require a complete rejection of established educational psychologies but may be used in conjunction with them" [**18, p. 7**]. Clark states that "transpersonal education, like science, is concerned with knowledge and discovery of truth. It does not, however, limit the search for truth to objectively verifiable measurement, prediction, and control" [**2, p. 1**]. Roberts goes even further and suggests that in addition to the affective, cognitive, and psychomotor domains, educators should recognize a fourth one—transpersonal [18].

Transpersonal education, like any theory, is a mixture of old and new. Clark's phrase, "rediscovering transpersonal education," is particularly apt [2]. The philosophical tenets of transpersonal education can be traced back to Aristotle, Shakespeare, and Kant. If Emerson were alive today, he would almost certainly be a transpersonal activist. Transpersonal education, of course, proposes some new terminology. It has also provided a common meeting ground for Western and Eastern psychologies. But basically, as Clark noted, transpersonal education is a rediscovery rather than a discovery. Hence, what is different or new is not transpersonal education but societal attitudes toward it. Roberts alludes to this.

> While men have thought about these areas [altered states of consciousness, self-transcendence, psychic phenomena] for millenia, transpersonal psychology is studying their psychological aspects scientifically, rather than relegating them to the realms of religion, mysticism, or the occult. [18, p. 191]

Scholars have at last displayed a serious interest in the transpersonal field. More important for transpersonal education, so has the general public. For the first time, the seeds of transpersonal education have fallen on fertile ground.

Why has contemporary society become receptive to transpersonal education and undertaken its nurture and growth? There are two basic reasons for this: individual alienation and the loss of established authority. Our alienation or estrangement in a modern society is not a recent phenomenon; it is primarily the product of mass culture and advanced technology. The essence of this concept, which was first developed by Hegel, is that the world (nature, things, others, and ourselves) has become alien to us. No longer do we experience ourselves as thinking, feeling, loving subjects of our own acts but as objects embodied only in the things we have created. We are in touch with ourselves only in our surrender to the products of creation [4]. Rollo May does not use the word "alienation," but his analysis fits perfectly.

> Is not one of the central problems of modern Western man that he experiences himself as without significance as an individual? Let us focus on that aspect of his image of himself, which is his doubt whether he can act and his half-aware conviction that even if he did act it would do no

> good. . . . Self-doubt . . . reflects the tremendous technolog-
> ical power that surges up every moment about him to dwarf
> overwhelmingly his own puny efforts. [**12, pp. 25–26**]

Because the development of our intellectual capacities has far out-
stripped the development of our emotions, we feel powerless against,
and thus alienated from, our world. As Erich Fromm put it, man's
brain lives in the twentieth century but his heart is still in the Stone
Age [**5**].

Prescribed authority made estrangement tolerable, but the recent loss of confidence in religious and political institutions has cast
modern humanity adrift with a profound and confused sense of loss.
According to Peter Marin:

> It is a condition of the soul, an absolute loss and yearning
> for the world. One can become anything—but nothing
> makes much sense. Adults have managed to evade it, have
> hesitated on its edges, have clung to one another and to
> institutions, to beliefs in "the system," to law and order. But
> now none of that coheres, and the young seem unprotected
> by it all, and what we have evaded and even celebrated in
> metaphor has become, for a whole generation, a kind of
> daily emotional life. [**11, p. 72**]

It is this "condition of the soul," the realization of the individual as the
only authority that gives meaning to life, that has prompted a reaching out for transpersonalism. Actually, the reach is not out but in. We
have turned to ourselves in the search for significance.

> Seldom has mankind been so bereft of believable external
> authority and so much in need of finding new myths to
> provide an image of the universe which accords with cur-
> rent knowledge. . . . It is by turning inward, therefore, that
> individuals are now seeking to feel at home in the universe
> rather than alienated in the world. [**2, p. 2**]

In his provocative book **Without Marx or Jesus**, Jean-François
Revel contends that America is undergoing a cultural revolution
based on the rejection of a society motivated by profit, dominated
exclusively by economic considerations, ruled by the spirit of compe-
tition, and subjected to the mutual aggressiveness of its members. If
this revolution is successful, human beings will become the masters
rather than the servants of technology and will find worth in themselves. Within the revolution, Revel sees the potential for a humanistic counterculture that will actually embody equality and justice [**16**].
While Revel may have been unduly optimistic, there is no question
that the counterculture revolution was instrumental in modifying
American attitudes and receptivity toward transpersonalism. The
time is not ripe for the educational radicalism of Goodman and Etz-

ioni, but the growing number of public schools using various forms of altered states of consciousness reveals an increasing acceptance of transpersonal education.

Teilhard de Chardin views Revel's cultural revolution as a cosmic revolution. In **The Phenomenon of Man**, he speaks of truth as a developing reality dependent on man's participation and reflection. Ever since man's evolution as the only "self-conscious being," truth, in a sense, is no longer objective. To this paleontologist-priest, man's evolutionary leap into a self-conscious mode ("I know that I am") has caused truth to assume a subjective existence. Evolution does not progress alone but progresses in interaction with man [22]. The phrase "the time is ripe" takes on nuances more powerful than ever before, for only man can allow the time to be ripe. Only man, freely accepting the possibility that truth has an intuitive, subjective, as well as a linear, objective, existence, can allow truth to be discovered and even created by acceptance of and participation in transpersonal learning.

Teilhard de Chardin also posits the existence of a noosphere of thought that is created by the pooling of man's intellectual energies [21]. According to his theory, all existing "life" (animal, vegetable,

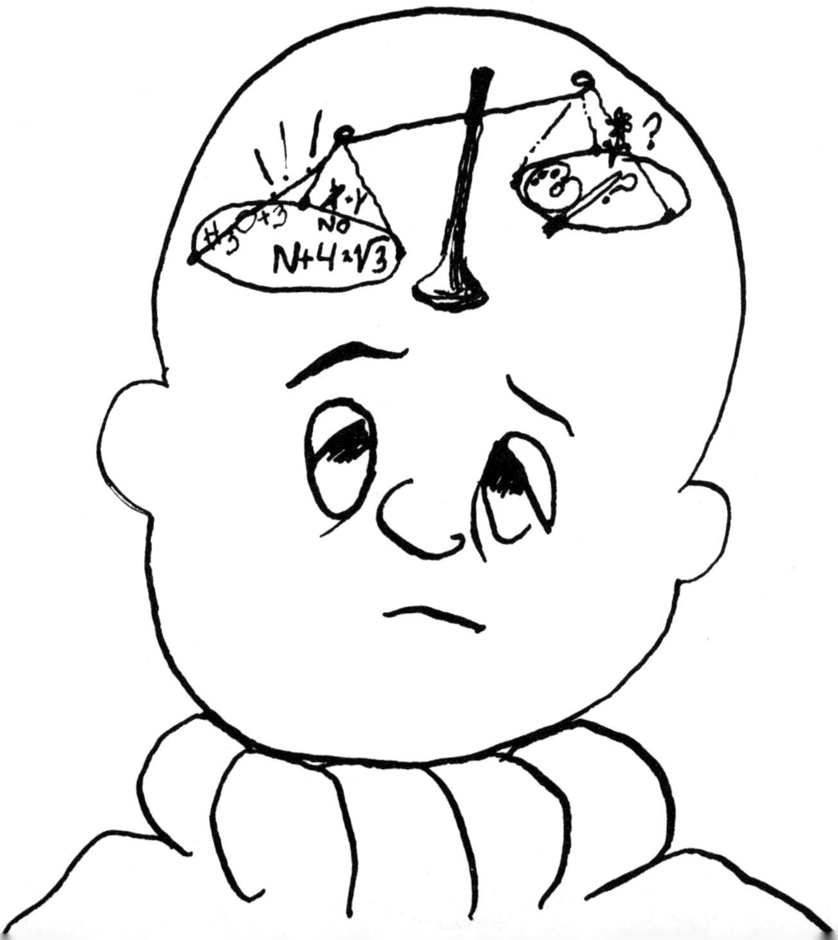

and mineral) possesses an inner energy—the "within" and an outer energy—the "without." We experience the "without" of existence daily, but we are often unaware of the "within." These two basic sources emit energy waves of varying intensities, depending on the events that surround them. For example, a plant that experiences treatment conducive to growth will emit energy waves strong enough to be measured and possibly strong enough to affect the atmosphere. The same is true of humanity. Producing thoughts that are pleasant and harmonious, we fill the immediate environment with a pleasant energy force. Human thought combines to form and feed the noosphere. Evolution contributes to this pool of thought and each age of man affects and is affected by the existent pool created by his ancestors. Jung speaks of a relational mode with the past that at times strikes nuances similar to the Teilhardian noosphere [7]. Such a construct of man immersed in a thought pool, a ripening intellectual milieu, has a bearing on the future of transpersonal learning. Its continuance is related to the openness of our age, to the possibility that cosmic consciousness may exist and that man's acceptance of a transpersonal mode of learning has worth.

Altered states of awareness or consciousness have a central, but not exclusive, importance to transpersonal education in general and to classroom teaching in particular. An individual's awareness of his

or her environment is in a constant state of fluctuation. Any perceived stimuli may alter this state. A meaningful stimulus will modify, if only momentarily, an individual's awareness. The most potent modulating influences are those that act directly on the brain. Drugs are very powerful external modulators of awareness. Those states of the organism that result in light sleep and dreaming are equally powerful internal modulators of awareness [23]. James described altered states of consciousness in the following manner:

> Our normal waking consciousness, rational consciousness as we call it, is but one special type of consciousness, whilst all about it, parted from it by the filmiest of screens, there lie potential forms of consciousness entirely different. We may go through life without suspecting their existence; but apply the requisite stimulus, and at a touch they are there

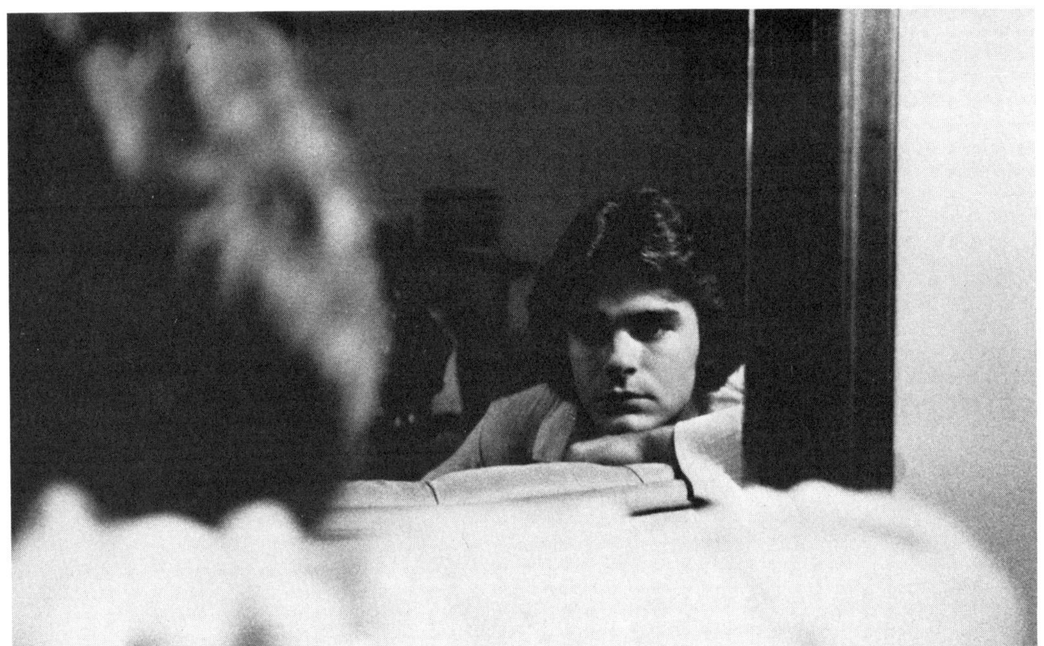

PHOTO BY LINDA GITS

in all their completeness, definite types of mentality which probably somewhere have their field of application and adaptation. No account of the universe in its totality can be final which leaves these other forms of consciousness quite disregarded. How to regard them is the question—for they are so discontinuous with ordinary consciousness. Yet they may determine attitudes though they cannot furnish formulas, and open a region though they fail to give a map. At any rate, they forbid a premature closing of our accounts with reality. [**6, p. 298**]

Ludwig's description is more succinct but equally vague. He defines an altered state of consciousness as any mental state representing a sufficient deviation in subjective experience or psychological functioning from certain general norms for an individual during alert, waking consciousness [**10**].

Drug-induced alterations of consciousness have both legal and social limitations. In some instances they produce negative side effects. Thus, transpersonal education utilizes nondrug methods of exploring and controlling consciousness. Relaxation, fantasy-imagery, dreams, suggestology-hypnosis, and meditation are some of the consciousness alterants currently being used in the classroom.

Relaxation and fantasy-imagery are probably the most widely used transpersonal techniques. Roberts recommends a combination of relaxation and fantasy journeys. This method allows students to intuitively integrate information in their minds at a preverbal level and to facilitate subsequent cognitive recall. Roberts reports impressive results from classroom teachers who have used this technique [18]. Hayes has demonstrated that dreams can be excellent aids in teaching creative writing [8]. Meditation, particularly transcendental meditation, has become almost commonplace in some public schools; the Illinois State Legislature passed a resolution encouraging schools to consider the use of transcendental meditation [17]. Lozanov's Institute of Suggestology in Sofia, Bulgaria has achieved such dramatic results in foreign language instruction that it has attracted international attention. In suggestopaedia, students relax in comfortable reclining chairs and breathe deeply. The relaxation techniques are adapted from yoga and are designed to increase the powers of concentration. Lozanov has found that his system speeds up the assimilation of a foreign language and greatly reduces the fatigue of four-hour class sessions [1].

Because of its recent development, transpersonal education is characterized largely by hazy contours, undefined features that can be both frustrating and exhilarating. This book is an attempt to further delineate transpersonal dimensions and to apply them to education. The subsequent chapters discuss five states of altered awareness and their application to classroom instruction.

REFERENCES

1. Bancroft, Jane W. "Foreign Language Teaching in Bulgaria." **Canadian Modern Language Review**, March 1972, pp. 9–13.
2. Clark, Frances V. "Rediscovering Transpersonal Education." **Journal of Transpersonal Education** 6 (1974): 1, 2.
3. Descartes, René. "Six Meditations." In **The Age of Reason**, edited by Stuart Hampshire. New York: Houghton Mifflin Co., 1956.
4. Fromm, Erich. **Beyond the Chains of Illusion**. New York: Simon & Schuster, 1962.
5. ______. **Escape from Freedom**. New York: Holt, Rinehart and Winston, 1965.
6. James, William. **The Varieties of Religious Experience**. New York: The New American Library, 1958.
7. Jung, Carl. **The Archetypes and the Collective Unconscious**. Bollingen Series, vol. 9, pt. 1. New York: Pantheon, 1959.
8. Hayes, Rosemary. "Do You Have Your Dream for English?" In **Four Psychologies Applied to Education**, edited by Thomas B. Roberts, pp. 417–420. Cambridge, Mass.: Schenkman Publishing Co., 1975.

9. Kant, Immanuel. **The Critique of Pure Reason**. London: Oxford University Press, 1881.

10. Ludwig, A. M. "Altered States of Consciousness." In **Altered States of Consciousness**, edited by Charles Tart. New York: John Wiley & Sons, 1969.

11. Marin, Peter. "Children of the Apocalypse." **Saturday Review**, 19, September, 1970, p. 72.

12. May, Rollo. **Psychology and the Human Dilemma**. Princeton: D. Van Nostrand Co., 1967.

13. Ornstein, Robert E. **The Psychology of Consciousness**. New York: The Viking Press, 1972.

14. Plato. "Phaedo." In **The Dialogues of Plato**. Jowett translation. New York: Washington Square Press, 1963.

15. Redmond, Hugh. "A Pioneer Program in Transpersonal Education." **Journal of Transpersonal Psychology** 6 (1974): 8–10.

16. Revel, Jean-François. **Without Marx or Jesus**. New York: Doubleday & Co., 1970.

17. Roberts, Thomas, and Clark, Frances. **Transpersonal Psychology in Education**. Bloomington, Ind.: Phi Delta Kappa Educational Foundation, 1975.

18. Roberts, Thomas B. "Transpersonal: The New Educational Psychology." **Phi Delta Kappan**, November 1974, p. 191.

19. Samples, Robert E. "Are You Teaching Only One Side of the Brain?" **Learning**, February 1975, pp. 24–28.

20. ______. "Learning With the Whole Brain." **Human Behavior**, February 1975, pp. 16–23.

21. Teilhard de Chardin, Pierre. **The Divine Milieu**. New York: Harper & Row, 1960.

22. ______. **The Phenomenon of Man**. New York: Harper & Row, 1962.

23. Teyler, Timothy J. **Altered States of Awareness**. San Francisco: W. H. Freeman and Co., 1954.

Since the early 1960s, a growing amount of scientific evidence has uncovered a new direction in the management of stress. At universities, medical schools, and other research institutions, investigators are looking seriously into the formal development of relaxation skills for daily living in a stress-filled society. The gist of the work is that the various methods of "letting go" (mental and physical relaxation techniques) have measurable and beneficial effects on such stress conditions as high blood pressure, migraine or tension headaches, learning ability and memory, and social and business skills [**4, p. 74**]. By reducing anxiety, relaxation has been shown to be useful in improving test scores [**3**], sports performance [**4**], and social skills [**1**]. In fact, relaxation seems to be an integral part of nearly any task. There is a paradox in the need to relax thoroughly before lifting a huge weight, taking part in a critical meeting, or performing an intricate surgery.

The definition of relaxation is at once simple and complex. Popularly, it is considered to be a state of "letting go." Webster defines it as "the act of making less tense or rigid; a recreative state or activity" [**9, p. 723**].

In 1920 Hans Berger, an Austrian psychiatrist, found that sensitive recording equipment (later named the electroencephalograph, or EEG) could detect the presence of exceedingly small voltages in the brain. He divided brain waves into four groups, identifying each with a Greek letter [**4, p. 190**]. These are presented in the following table.

	BRAIN WAVES			
	DELTA	THETA	ALPHA	BETA
FREQUENCY in cycles per second (Hertz)	1-3.5	4-7	8-12	13-30

Delta waves are produced during sleep. The theta wave occurs during deep reverie and seems to be associated with artistic and intellectual creation. Beta waves accompany the state of ordinary, eyes-open attention. Of all these brain waves, alpha holds a certain preeminent position. It seems to be a necessary element that precedes entry into all the other wave conditions. Hence, before entering a delta condition of sleep, a person must first relax, or enter the alpha state. Paradoxically, alpha also is a prerequisite for entering the theta condition of creative thought. Consequently, the alpha state, or calm relaxation, acts as a crucial doorway to both creative endeavors and deep sleep.

For the purposes of this text, relaxation will be discussed as "letting-go" techniques that enable a person to enter the relaxed state of alpha. How this state is used depends on specific need. Relaxation can be employed as a stress-reduction tool, a creativity-enhancing device, or a simple self-awareness exercise. Whatever the result, its use is beneficial for all of daily existence.

The discussion and experience of mental and physical relaxation are related to all other aspects of this book. Since relaxation, or the alpha state, precedes the other altered states of consciousness, the specific activities related to relaxation tend to overlap and contain elements of the other altered states [7].

APPLICATION OF RELAXATION TO EDUCATION

Education for both young and old has centered on knowledge about the external, material, and social world. Even philosophy, the study of existence, has focused on man or life as ideas to be discerned from some rational system, examining these basic constructs as objects. For too long the dictum "know thyself" has been followed according to purely rational, objective procedures.

Such a quantifiable, concrete, and objective approach toward learning has been (and continues to be) highly successful. It is limited, however, for it fails to incorporate the subjective, the experiential, the present moment, which has more than an objective, concrete aspect. There is an untapped area of knowing yet to be explored—that of coming in touch with the inner self, the subjective moments of emotion, feeling, and intuition.

The immediate response of many educators to such a subjective approach toward learning can take two forms. The first is that of the well-trained skeptic, who thinks that if knowledge is to be valid, it must be linear, logical, rational, and objective; hence, the entire task of pursuing subjective learning is meaningless. The second possible reaction is that of the uncertain but interested thinker: The idea is exciting and seems worthy of investigation but the **how** is just too complex. Methods are vague and difficult to use in the classroom setting because the teacher has not had the opportunity to explore them or to become comfortable in using them.

Piaget emphasized the latter point throughout his entire analysis of cognitive development [2]. Repeatedly, he asserts that before any learning can take place, no matter how elevated the level, the learner must first be secure or comfortable in the learning. It seems appropriate, therefore, to use relaxation techniques as an entry point in the development of subjective or right-hemisphere learning.

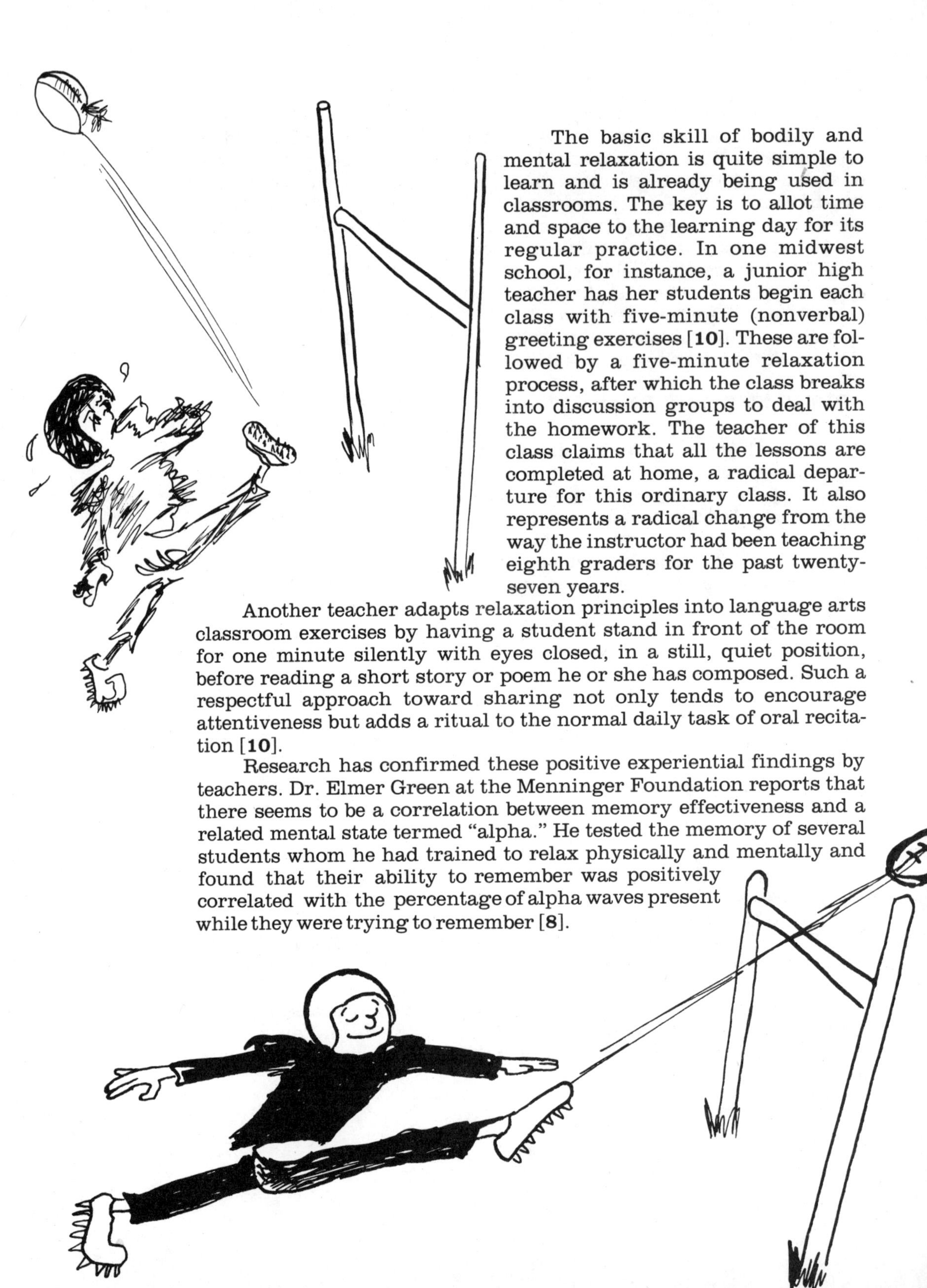

The basic skill of bodily and mental relaxation is quite simple to learn and is already being used in classrooms. The key is to allot time and space to the learning day for its regular practice. In one midwest school, for instance, a junior high teacher has her students begin each class with five-minute (nonverbal) greeting exercises [10]. These are followed by a five-minute relaxation process, after which the class breaks into discussion groups to deal with the homework. The teacher of this class claims that all the lessons are completed at home, a radical departure for this ordinary class. It also represents a radical change from the way the instructor had been teaching eighth graders for the past twenty-seven years.

Another teacher adapts relaxation principles into language arts classroom exercises by having a student stand in front of the room for one minute silently with eyes closed, in a still, quiet position, before reading a short story or poem he or she has composed. Such a respectful approach toward sharing not only tends to encourage attentiveness but adds a ritual to the normal daily task of oral recitation [10].

Research has confirmed these positive experiential findings by teachers. Dr. Elmer Green at the Menninger Foundation reports that there seems to be a correlation between memory effectiveness and a related mental state termed "alpha." He tested the memory of several students whom he had trained to relax physically and mentally and found that their ability to remember was positively correlated with the percentage of alpha waves present while they were trying to remember [8].

Musicians, philosophers, artists, and athletes have been shown to be prolific alpha-wave producers. Jodi Lawrence, a researcher in the field of relaxation, claims that Albert Einstein was a strong producer of such relaxation waves, particularly when he theorized [5]. Creativity and alpha activity, relief from anxiety, improved ability to meet the world's stresses, the capacity to learn and absorb information faster and better—all seem to be related to relaxation. Educators can either ignore or inhibit this necessary ingredient of learning or enhance it by classroom implementation.

SPECIFIC TEACHING STRATEGIES AND TECHNIQUES

Relaxation is a versatile skill. It has as many uses as people have needs. It can be regarded as an end in itself—"I just need to relax"—or it can be employed as a tool to accomplish something else. No matter what the activity, a relaxed body and mind seems to help.

Body Relaxation

This activity, done while lying on the floor, helps quiet the body by dissolving muscle tension. Although this is a long exercise, children can, with practice, reach the state of relaxation instantly. For this and later activities, it is nice to have mats or a rug on the floor.

"This is an activity that can help us learn to relax our bodies and minds by tensing and releasing muscles. We cannot be tense and relaxed at the same time, so if we learn to relax we can avoid wasting energy through muscle tension. If you ever feel tense, while asking a question or taking a test or any time, you can use the feeling of relaxation to feel better.

"Let's begin by lying on our backs on the floor and not touching anyone else. Wiggle around a little until you find a way of lying down that is completely comfortable. Now close your eyes and think of your hands. Feel the bones inside them, feel the muscles that move the bones, feel the weight of them on the floor. Now make a fist with your hands and clench tightly. Hold your hands tightly (ten seconds). Now relax and feel the soothing, tingling feeling of relaxation come into your hands.

(Pause: ten seconds or so between instructions)

"Now draw up your arms and tighten your biceps as tight as you can. Hold them tightly (ten seconds). Now relax and feel the tension drain out of your arms.

(Pause)

"Shrug your shoulders now, pushing them as if to push them up through your ears. Hold them tightly there (ten seconds). Now let them go and feel all the tension drain out of your body.

(Pause)

"Continuing to keep your eyes closed, open your mouth as far as it will go, stretching the muscles at the corners of your mouth. Hold it tightly (ten seconds). Relax and enjoy the tingling feeling as the tension dissolves in your mouth.

(Pause)

"Now press your tongue against the roof of your mouth and tighten your jaw muscles. Press tightly and hold it (ten seconds). Now let go and relax. Let the peaceful feeling of relaxation flow through your body.

(Pause)

"Now wrinkle your nose and make a face. Scrunch up your face tightly and hold it (ten seconds). Relax now, feeling the tension flow out of your face.

(Pause)

"Now tighten the muscles of your chest, stomach, and abdomen. Draw all the muscles in tightly and hold them tense (ten seconds). Now let them go, feeling the soothing feeling of relaxation pour in.

(Pause)

"Now tense the muscles of your thighs by straightening your legs. Hold them tightly (ten seconds). Now relax your thighs—let all the tension drain out of them.

(Pause)

"Now tense the backs of your legs by straightening your legs. Hold your legs tensely (ten seconds). Now relax them and let all of the tension go.

(Pause)

"Now tense your feet by curling the toes. Keep them curled tightly (ten seconds). Now relax your toes and feel the delicious feeling of relaxation come into your feet.

(Pause)

"Your whole body is feeling loose and relaxed now. Feel yourself completely supported by the floor and breathe deeply, and as you breathe in, let each breath fill your body with deeper and deeper feelings of relaxation.

(Pause)

"See if there are any places of tension left in your body. If you feel tense in some area, take a deep breath and send the breath to that place. Fill that tense area with breath, and let the feeling of tension leave your body.

(Pause)

"Let the soothing feeling of relaxation fill your body. Each breath takes you deeper and deeper into relaxation.

(Pause: thirty seconds to one minute)

"Now you will be coming out of relaxation in a moment, and you will feel rested and alert. I will count backward from ten to one, and as I do, feel your body becoming alert at your own rate.

"Ten, nine, eight, feel the alertness returning to your body. Seven, six, five, feel your toes and fingers begin to move. Four, three, move your arms and legs. Two, eyes, one, get up slowly, feeling completely rested and alert."

From Gay Hendricks and Russel Wills, **The Centering Book: Awareness Activities for Children, Parents, and Teachers**, ©1975, pp. 41–45. Reprinted by permission of Prentice-Hall, Englewood Cliffs, N.J.

28

SQUEEZE AND STRETCH. Here's an exercise that gives instant relaxation effectively. It uses planned stress or voluntary tension to provide relief from unconscious tension. Once again, it's nice to have mats or a rug on the floor.

"Sit on the floor, and see how small a space your body can occupy. Bend your knees, and encircle your arms around them, pressing your heels into your buttocks. Bury your face in your thighs.

"Then contract. Clench your fists, forearms, biceps. Bring your shoulders forward, and contract your belly. Scrunch up your face, so that it is as small as you can make it. Squeeze closed your toes, feet, calves, thighs, buttocks, eyes.

"Hold this position until it becomes absolutely unbearable, a minute at least. Keep tightening up muscles that ease loose.

"Now release—and instantly do the reverse exercise: Stretch; re-al-ly stretch, so that you occupy as much space as possible. Arch your back. Spread your toes and fingers. Pull apart your wrists, elbows, shoulders, your ankles, knees, and pelvic joints. Stretch your face. Open your eyes and mouth wide. Stick out your tongue.

"Hold for a minute or two. Release, and breathe deeply and slowly. A great wave of peace is almost certain to come over you.

"What's happened? Your body has gone from stress to strain to natural equilibrium. When you tense part of your body voluntarily and consciously, you can become aware of the tension and voluntarily let it go. Voluntary tensing, like the kind you've just done, can raise your unconscious tensions to a level of awareness. Thus, they may be relieved."

From **Growth Games**, pp. 136–137, copyright ©1970 by Howard R. Lewis and Harold S. Streitfeld. Reprinted by permission of Harcourt Brace Jovanovich, Inc. and Souvenir Press Ltd.

Breathing

The Greeks knew that breathing directly affects one's emotional state. The term "psyche" is derived from a Greek word that came to mean "soul" after it had originally meant "the vital breath." By controlling breathing, a person can learn to relax and control feelings [6].

LUNGS ALIVE.   This activity should be performed in a gymnasium or some other setting that permits noise.

Explain to the students that most of us are half breathers. They probably will find it a strain to take a full deep breath. To breathe lower into their lungs they need to exhale more deeply. Explain to the students that yelling helps get the old air out, along with held-in feelings. In order to use this fact have them slap their entire chest vigorously but not painfully. As they slap have the students yell "AHHHH" as loudly as possible. After half a minute or so let the yelling and slapping subside. Let them experience the effects and share them with one another.

Adapted from **Growth Games**, p. 127, copyright © 1970 by Howard R. Lewis and Harold S. Streitfeld. Reprinted by permission of Harcourt Brace Jovanovich, Inc. and Souvenir Press Ltd.

PILLOW FIGHT.   Another way to stimulate breathing in a group activity is to have a pillow fight. The pillows should be a good handful but small enough to be throwable.

For five to ten minutes, let the students hurl pillows at anyone in sight. Afterwards, have them quietly experience the exhilarating feeling of being alive and breathing deeply.

Adapted from **Growth Games**, p. 127, copyright © 1970 by Howard R. Lewis and Harold S. Streitfeld. Reprinted by permission of Harcourt Brace Jovanovich, Inc. and Souvenir Press Ltd.

FORCED-AIR BREATHING. Breathing forcibly like a bellows is often effective for relieving tension as well as for relaxing. Instruct the students in the following manner:

"Draw in as much air as you can through tightly pursed lips, as though you were breathing through a straw. Then push the air out, as though you were squeezing water from a sponge. Put your consciousness in parts of your body where there is blocking. Your concentration of thought will stimulate these parts and open them up to more feeling. Grunt, gasp, yell, as you breathe—the sounds are stimulating."

Bellowslike breathing can be invigorating in any position, at any time; it can be especially effective while arching back over a two-foot-high stool. Forcible breathing over a stool is especially good for freeing the pelvis. Combine the breathing and stretching with a rocking back and forth, similar to what a driver does to free a tire stuck in the snow.

Adapted from **Growth Games**, p. 127, copyright © 1970 by Howard R. Lewis and Harold S. Streitfeld. Reprinted by permission of Harcourt Brace Jovanovich, Inc. and Souvenir Press Ltd.

Centering

Students can be taught to relax quickly by contracting their "centers." This simple approach can be used in daily life when they need to relax, or when they feel "scattered" and need to pull themselves together. This activity can be done in any position.

"Today we will learn how to get in touch with our 'center.' Once we learn how to contact our center, we can use it to relax, to pull ourselves together when we feel scattered, and to feel better, even when we aren't feeling bad.

"Focus all of your attention on your center. Send all of your thoughts and feelings down to that point just below your naval.

(Pause: ten seconds)

"Now begin sending each breath all the way down to your center.

(Pause: ten seconds)

"Each time you breathe, send the breath to your center.

(Pause: ten seconds)

"Now that you know how to get in touch with your center, you can focus on that point when you feel nervous or angry, or whenever you want to feel better . . . it's always there when you need it."

From Gay Hendricks and Russel Wills, **The Centering Book: Awareness Activities for Children, Parents, and Teachers**, © 1975, pp. 24–25. Reprinted by permission of Prentice-Hall, Englewood Cliffs, N.J.

INSTANT CENTERING.   One of the reasons centering feels so good is that it clears our heads of scattered, cluttering thoughts. Here are several quick images to which young people have responded very well:

Have the students put all their thoughts in an elevator up in their heads. Then have them punch the button and send the elevator down to their centers.

Have the students imagine an hourglass inside them, the top in their heads, the bottom in their centers. Have them let the sand slowly fill up the bottom.

Have the students imagine a light shining out from their centers, and have them vary the intensity of the light.

From Gay Hendricks and Russel Wills, **The Centering Book: Awareness Activities for Children, Parents, and Teachers,** ©1975, pp. 25–26. Reprinted by permission of Prentice-Hall, Englewood Cliffs, N.J.

REFERENCES

1. Hendricks, Gay, and Wills, Russel. **The Centering Book: Awareness Activities for Children, Parents, and Teachers.** Englewood Cliffs, N.J.: Prentice-Hall, 1975.
2. Inhelder, B., and Piaget, J. **The Growth of Logical Thinking From Childhood to Adolescence**. New York: Basic Books, 1958.
3. Krippner, Stanley. "The Use of Hypnosis and the Improvement of Academic Achievement." **The Journal of Special Education** 4 (1970): 451–460.
4. Lamont, Kenneth, **Escape From Stress.** New York: G. P. Putnam, 1974.
5. Lawrence, Jodi. **Alpha Brain Waves.** New York: Nash Publishing Co. 1972.
6. Lewis, Howard, and Streitfeld, Harold. **Growth Games**. New York: Harcourt Brace Jovanovich, 1970.
7. Luthe, Wolfgang, ed. **Autogenic Therapy.** New York: Grune and Stratton Publishing, 1969.
8. Payne, Buryl. **Getting There Without Drugs.** New York: Ballantine Publishing Co. 1974.
9. Webster's Seventh New Collegiate Dictionary. New York: G. & C. Merriam Co., 1973.
10. Westheimer, Benjamin S. "Experiencing Education with EST." In **Four Psychologies Applied to Education**, edited by Thomas B. Roberts, pp. 528–536. Cambridge, Mass.: Schenkman Publishing Co., 1975.

Simply defined, imagery is seeing pictures in the mind, or, as Lawrence puts it, the ability to think in pictures; she characterizes it as a mental happening [11]. Hunter calls it a "sensory-like experiencing which occurs in the absence of appropriate sensory stimulation" [9, p. 184]. Jung describes imagery as the language of the unconscious that may be tapped through altered states of awareness [10]. Although most commonly regarded as a visual phenomenon, it may be auditory, kinesthetic, or a combination of sensory modalities. According to Doob, imagery is unrelated to social, cultural, or demographic factors and thus is found in all social and ethnic groups [5]. Ericka Fromm calls it a universal language [7]. It is generally believed to occur more often in children than adults; however, McKellar reports a survey of 500 adults in which more than 90 percent related instances of visual and auditory imagery and more than half reported instances of kinesthetic, tactile, gustatory, olfactory, and pain imagery [14].

Historically, imagery has been viewed as possessing significant survival value [5]. Recent research has revealed that fantasies about home and family gave American prisoners of war the incentive to endure torture and deprivation in North Vietnam [17]. Piaget was probably the first researcher to recognize the importance of make-believe in intellectual development. The methodological study of his own children revealed the importance of make-believe symbolism in bridging the gap between concrete experience and abstract thought [16].

Among modern theorists, the most generally acknowledged function of imagery is to act as a vehicle for coding information during the processes of thinking, reasoning, and remembering. The ability to visualize material is a powerful aid in retaining and recalling it, and training in visualization normally increases retention and

CURRICULUM LAB

recall [**4, p. 15**]. Bruner and Church have documented the importance of visualization in thinking and reasoning, especially among young children [**1; 2**]. Like Richardson, Hendricks and Wills suggest that imagery plays a useful, if not critical, role in certain forms of problem solving, such as complex spatial relationships [**8**]. Make-believe is not only a valuable way to improve cognitive skills; it is also a powerful tool for self-exploration and self-expression. Singer suggests that imagery helps people to be more creative and flexible in solving problems and improves their ability to postpone immediate self-gratification [**18**]. According to Clark, willed introversion is a classic device of creative genius [**3**].

APPLICATION OF IMAGERY TO EDUCATION

Imagery and fantasy can be used to facilitate many types of learning. Hendricks and Wills contend that imagery is crucial to education.

> Imagine trying to read without picturing things; doing a geometry problem without seeing the symbols in your head; or remembering without seeing the important implications. Inasmuch as imagery plays such a large role in education, it is surprising that the typical school curriculum does not contain activities that help students develop this skill. It becomes even more curious when we consider that practically every widely accepted educational goal, from divergent thinking to positive self-image, depends upon imagery. [**8, p. 93**]

Recent research findings show that imaginative play significantly helps children's intellectual development. Students who engage in fantasy are able to concentrate and to cope with frustration and anxiety better and tend to have more self-control. Singer found that when asked to make up stories, high fantasizers told more creative stories than low fantasizers [**18**]. In her research and psychotherapy, Freyberg found that disadvantaged five-year-olds made gains in attention span, self-control, and the ability to interact and communicate with other children after they had been trained to play more imaginatively [**6**]. She also found parental attitude to be the most significant differentiating variable between children with high and low imagination.

> A parent who has positive feelings about pretending and who encourages, demonstrates, and teaches it to his child in the preschool years, helps to develop this important skill in the youngsters. [**6, p. 63**]

Research by Pulaski revealed that children low in the ability to fantasize tend to be less creative and less flexible in their thinking and poorer at concentration [**17**]. Both Freyberg and Pulaski contend

that a teacher can be an important catalyst in developing and expanding a child's imagination. One way of accomplishing this is through the use of reading, story telling, role playing, and free-form materials [6, p. 17]. Westheimer related the experience of a teacher of the mentally retarded who led her students on an imaginary journey through their bodies. After eight sessions over a two-week period, their drawings of themselves showed marked improvement. Previously, their self drawings were only bloblike images with arms sticking out to the sides. After the imagery trips, their drawings included body details such as ankles, knees, and chins, and they depicted clothing details such as pants, belt buckles, and necklines. The spatial balance of their drawings also improved [20].

After using fantasy trips in his classroom, a junior high school teacher reported:

> If before [**EST**] I had three good classes and two disasters, it was the best I could hope for. Suddenly, I have five fantastic classes. I am confident, able to joke in class—a major change for me. I am at ease and able to do what I want to do in class without regard for the class's reactions . . . and they respond by doing three, four, sometimes five times the amount of work—all of it better quality. And all of this gets done after I use maybe a quarter or a third of the class time on some fantasy journey into a marshmallow or a potato chip. [**20, p. 533**]

In an experimental study at Central Michigan University, Lovinger found a significant improvement in language skills among four- and five-year-olds, following twenty-five weeks of make-believe play. This was a well-controlled study utilizing a pretest, post-test, and control-experimental group design [**12**]. Westheimer reports that another teacher observed:

> I would start each Monday with a guided fantasy journey. It sounds silly, I mean, to take them on an imaginary walk through a foreign country, or to a beach, or into a color when I teach math to junior-high-age students. But they responded. They settled down, seemed more intent . . . and dammit, they just did better math. The class average shot up 30 percent in about six weeks. [**20, p. 530**]

Most of the teachers who have used imagery successfully to improve cognitive skills have also found an improvement in classroom behavior.

SPECIFIC TEACHING STRATEGIES AND TECHNIQUES

Active imagination and fantasy have endless possibilities in the classroom. Guidance may be very specific and detailed, or the teacher may give brief preliminary instructions and permit the students to go their own way. Generally, introductory work with imagery should be quite specific until students become familiar with their capacity to fantasize. Exercises in guided fantasy should be preceded by a short period of relaxation.

The following simple exercise is recommended by Clark as an effective way to enable students to recognize their capacity for vivid imagery:

> **"Imagine that you are standing in front of a blank screen, and on the screen you see a picture of a lemon. As you look at the lemon, it becomes three dimensional and you are able to hold it in your hand. Notice the texture of**

the skin, all the little dots on the surface, the bump at the one end and the place where it was attached to the tree at the other end. Smell the lemon and put it down on the table. Now pick up a knife and, very slowly, cut the lemon, noticing every movement. When the lemon is cut, look at the inside of it, noticing the white part, the sections inside, and the texture of each part. Now squeeze one part slightly and taste it. (Pause) When you are ready, open your eyes." [3, p. 504]

Following this introductory exercise, physiological changes such as salivation and other dramatic sensations should be discussed. Sharing these experiential feelings is a convincing way for students to develop imagery confidence. During these discussions, it is very important for the teacher to display an attitude of acceptance [3].

PHOTO BY PEG REYNOLDS

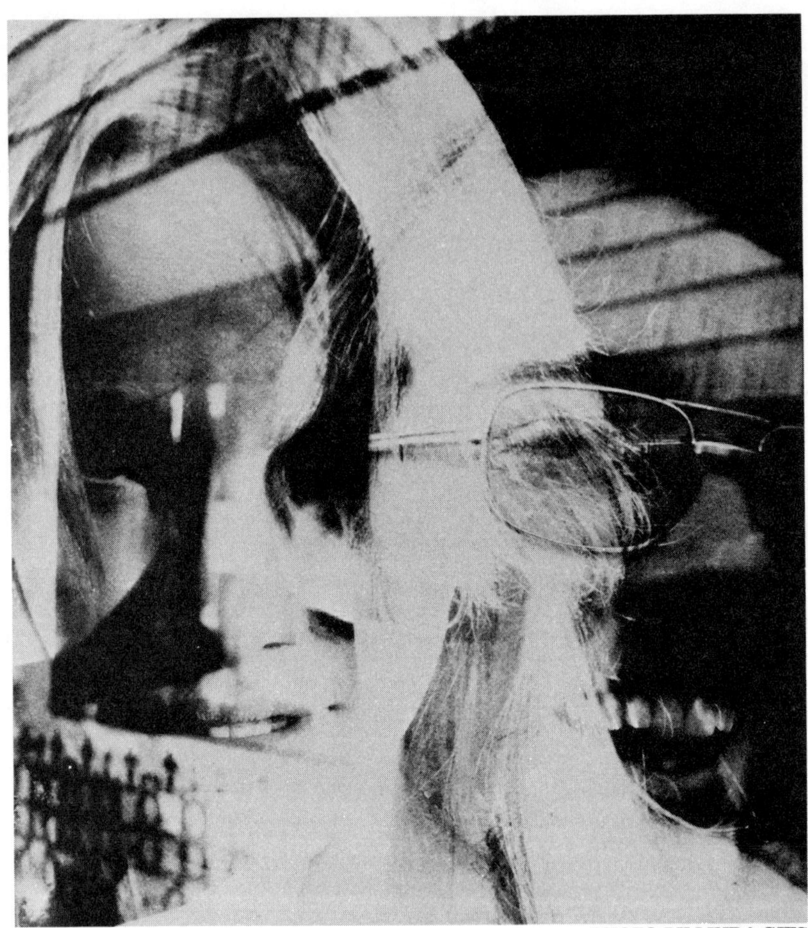

PHOTO BY LINDA GITS

The imagery exercises described in this section may be used in any classroom exactly as presented or may be adapted for different age levels and subjects. Teachers have found some of the techniques remarkably effective in developing class cohesion, cooperation, and a sense of community. The open communication results in better comprehension and retention regardless of the nature of the subject matter. Many of the basic awareness exercises demonstrate the scientific method of observation and hypothesis testing of reality through experimentation. Role playing of historic conflicts not only can improve historical comprehension but also can provide experiential understanding of conflict resolution. Some of the exercises may be used in art, drama, or creative writing classes to enhance artistic self-expression. It is not uncommon for teachers who have used imagery exercises in their classrooms to report an improvement in their students' self-concept. The resulting self-confidence is a valuable gain in any class.

The following imagery exercises have been collected from several different sources. All of them have been used in public school classrooms. The teachers who used them have reported positive cognitive and affective gains.

Fantasy Journeys

"Imagine yourself as a seed in the earth which begins to germinate and grow. What kind of plant are you? How do you experience each of the seasons as the growth process continues? How do you experience being the roots of this plant? The stem? The flower or the leaves? What does the sunlight feel like? The rain? The wind? Imagine that as this plant you are sensitive to everything in your environment."

"You are standing before a closed door. Over the door is written a word. (The guide may suggest a specific word or let the subject imagine his own.) Someone you know brings you a key. You open the door and go in."

"You are at the foot of a mountain which you are prepared to climb. The ascent is difficult but you are able to overcome the various obstacles which you encounter on the way. Take your time and keep going until you reach the top of the mountain."

"You are walking up a mountain path and you see a cave. You enter the cave and see a fire glowing deep within. As you approach the fire, you see a very old person seated by the fire. This person is very wise and will answer any question you ask and will give you a significant object to bring back with you."

"You are standing at a crossroads. There is a sign at the crossroads. You read the sign and choose to follow one of the roads. Notice what you are taking with you on this journey. Follow the road of your choice and see where it leads."

"You are in a meadow. Explore the meadow and get to know it. Notice the size of the meadow and the weather. Someone is going to come into your meadow. When that person is with you, imagine that you become him or her and see yourself and the meadow through his or her eyes. Experience as fully as you can what it would be like to be the other person's body. Become yourself again, and say goodbye to the other person."

PHOTO BY LINDA GITS

"Imagine that you are a body of water. Choose a body of water which symbolizes the way you feel at this time. Experience the cycles of light and dark and be aware of any life forms existing within you. Imagine the process of evaporation as the sun warms you, and the process of cooling and precipitation."

"Imagine that you are going on a journey into space. As you move away from the earth, your perception of time and space is altered, allowing you to perceive reality in a totally new way. As you continue to move out through avenues of stars, your wisdom and understanding increase. When you return in your localized awareness, you will remember the insight you gained from this perspective."

"You are entering a room of mirrors. Every surface reflects a different image of you. Look at each one and get to know it."

PHOTO BY JILL STEFANI

42

"Imagine that you are a very young infant. Notice your surroundings, and how it feels to be where you are. You do not have to rely on memory. Simply imagine what it is like to be a very small child. Going forward in time, imagine what it is like to be five years old. How do you experience the world at the age of five? How does it feel to be five? Going on to the age of twelve now, what is it like to be twelve years old? How do you see the world at age twelve? Going on now to age twenty-five, how does it feel to be you at twenty-five? How do you experience the world at twenty-five? Going on now to age forty, how does it feel to be you at forty? How do you feel about yourself and the world at forty? Now imagine that you are sixty-five years old. How do you see your life from the point of view of sixty-five years? Imagine now that you are very, very old. Soon you will die. Allow yourself to imagine your own death, and rest a while after that experience. Imagine now that you can be reborn as anything you choose. When you feel ready to open your eyes, imagine that you are seeing the world for the first time."

The Search

"I want you to imagine that you are searching for something that is very important to you. You may have some idea of what it is that you are looking for, or you may not. You do know, however, that what you are searching for is very important to you, and that your life will be somehow incomplete until you find it. Where are you now, as you begin this search? . . . Where do you go? . . . And how do you search? . . . What happens to you? . . . Notice what obstacles or delays are in your way. . . . And be aware of how you encounter these obstacles and how you deal with them. What alternatives do you try? . . . Continue on this search for a while. Discover more about it, and see how close you can come to your goal. . . . You may find that the search changes in some way as you proceed. What do you find as you continue your search? . . . Even if you have not yet reached the goal of your search, you may have discovered more about what you are searching for. You may even be able to see it in the distance, even though something prevents you from reaching it. Whatever your situation, try to discover more about the object of your search. Whether you have found what you are looking for, or can only see it, or can only imagine what it is like, examine it carefully . . . and be aware of your feelings toward it. . . . What is your goal like? . . . And what would reaching your goal do for you? . . . Is it this goal itself that you want, or is it a means—a way of getting something else that you want? . . . If this goal could speak to you now, what would it say to you? . . . And what would you say to it? . . . Talk to it for a while, and see if you can learn more from it. . . .

"Now return to your existence in this room and stay quietly with your experience for a while."

From John O. Stevens, **Awareness: Exploring, Experimenting, Experiencing**, (Moab, Utah: Real People Press, 1971), pp. 185–186. Reprinted by permission of John O. Stevens.

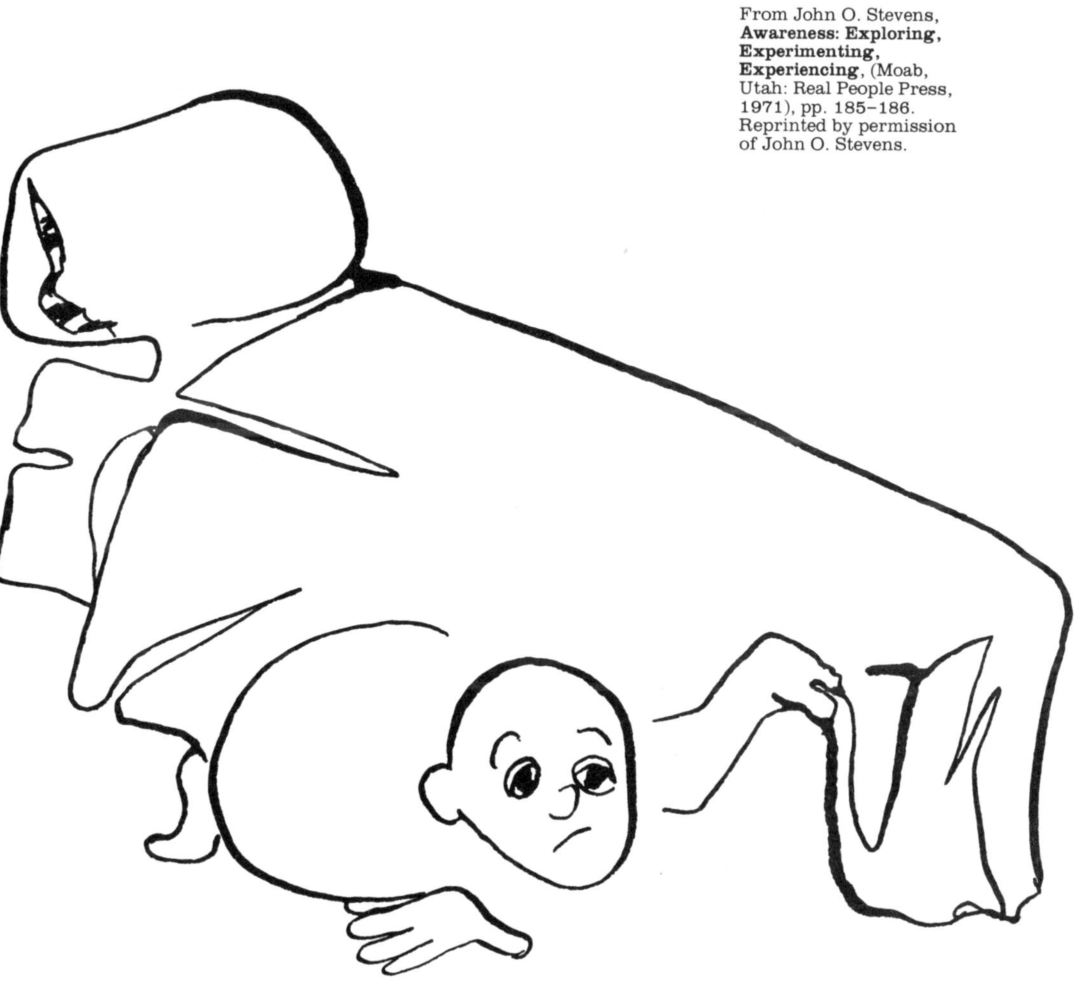

One-Way Feeling Glasses

Gerald Weinstein will enter, for example, a sixth grade inner city classroom with a box full of old dimestore glasses. In one classroom he explained to the children that he had very special "one-way feeling glasses." "When you put these on, you see things suspiciously." He asked for a volunteer to try on the glasses. A small boy in the front of the classroom came up and put them on. He looked around and smiled. When asked what he saw through the suspicious glasses, he replied, "I wonder why you're here today, and the teacher is out loafing or goofing off?" Gerald Weinstein told him, "That's exactly the way suspicious glasses work!" The boy looked around the room, and said, "I wonder if those two boys in the back of the room are talking about me." Several other children used the suspicious glasses with equal success.

Gerald Weinstein then pulled another pair of glasses out of the box and said, "These are 'I know they really care about me no matter what they say or do glasses.'" Several children tried them on with revealing results.

One of the pairs of glasses, the "self-righteous glasses," provided some interesting results. When asked who might wear "self-righteous glasses," one child replied, "Batman." Another said the counselor. When asked more about this, he replied that whenever you go in to see the counselor, he asks, "What trouble have you been in now?" Another said, "The principal." When asked what the opposite of "self-righteous glasses" might be, one student replied, "'People are not too different from me' glasses."

When the students in the class all put on "strong point glasses" and looked around at their fellow students, the classroom became alive with feeling as students began honestly telling their associates, in most cases for the first time, about their strengths. A warm pleasant feeling seemed to spread among these ghetto-hardened children as they heard reinforcing feedback about their strong points from others in the class.

When asked what kind of glasses "a new kid" coming into the class ought to have, the students replied "power glasses" to make it through the struggle. A new student in the class emphatically agreed, and this touched off a discussion on how he had been accepted by the others. This ended with the conclusion that he was not definitely a member of the group.

The author has used the "strong point glasses" technique with graduate students with amazing results. After having each student, in turn, put on "strong point glasses" and give each of the others' strong points, the author passed around a hand mirror and asked each student to tell what he saw in the mirror, still wearing his "strong point glasses." This gave students the rare opportunity to openly and honestly state what they felt their strong points to be. It was a most intimate, warm, and satisfying experience for the entire group of 15 students.

This technique of one-way feeling glasses has infinite variation and application limited only by the teacher's imagination and self-enlightenment.

From Harold C. Lyon, Jr., **Learning to Feel—Feeling to Learn** (Columbus, Ohio: Charles E. Merrill Publishing Co., 1971), pp. 146–147. Reprinted by permission of Charles E. Merrill Publishing Co.

Flower

"Close your eyes and tell your muscles to relax. Tell your arms and hands to let go . . . now your legs . . . now your chest . . . your face. And as you enjoy the calm feeling of resting in the darkness, imagine a closed flower in your mind. And as you imagine this flower, see it slowly begin to open . . . the petals beginning to spread and separate . . . and a beautiful flower opens in your mind. And as your mind becomes filled with the beauty of the flower, you can imagine the rest of the bush: the leaves and branches being your arms, and the roots reaching down through your center into the ground, connecting you solidly with the earth.

(Pause: ten seconds)

"And whenever you want to feel good, you can remember the feeling of the flower opening . . . the feeling of the roots connecting you with the ground, helping you feel solid and complete. And now let's return to the present, feeling rested and calm, relaxed and alert."

From Gay Hendricks and Russel Wills, **The Centering Book: Awareness Activities for Children, Parents, and Teachers,** ©1975, pp. 98–99. Reprinted by permission of Prentice-Hall, Inc., Englewood Cliffs, N.J.

PHOTO BY PEG REYNOLDS

"We will be taking a journey through inner space and you can begin by closing your eyes and letting your body relax . . . letting go your toes . . . your feet . . . your legs . . . relaxing your stomach . . . your chest . . . your arms . . . your face . . . your mind . . . and your fingertips. And as you listen to my voice, let it take you deeper and deeper into that feeling of relaxation in which you feel soothed, calm, and peaceful. And as you feel calmer and calmer, imagine that there is a calm, still lake down in the center of your body . . . a peaceful, clear lake filled with fresh, still water. And now as you feel still and calm as this lake, drop a pebble into the center of the lake and feel the ripples spreading slowly and smoothly from the center.

(Pause: thirty seconds)

"You can return to that feeling of stillness within you whenever you would like to feel still and peaceful. Now let's return our attention to right here, opening our eyes to the light and feeling refreshed and calm."

From Gay Hendricks and Russel Wills, **The Centering Book: Awareness Activities for Children, Parents, and Teachers,** ©1975, pp. 102–103. Reprinted by permission of Prentice-Hall, Inc., Englewood Cliffs, N.J.

PHOTO BY PEG REYNOLDS

"Form groups of three to five people, and don't talk. In a moment, I'm going to ask the people in each group to come together and become a machine. As you come together to become this machine, I want each person to make sounds, movements, and physical contact with at least two other people. Ham it up a little and enjoy yourself. Don't talk, don't plan, and do remember the three essential ingredients: sounds, movements, and physical contact with at least two other people. Now come together and become a washing machine for about four minutes. . . .

"Now stop, close your eyes for a minute and get in touch with your physical existence. . . . What is going on inside you? . . . How do you feel? . . . I want you to become aware of how you express yourself and how you interact with the others in your group machine. To what extent did you want to plan and organize the machine? To what extent did you feel self-conscious, uncomfortable, and unable to let yourself go? How did the others in your group enter into being the washing machine? Did they participate with a lot of energy and vitality, or were they hesitant and somewhat paralyzed? . . . Who was most energetic and involved, and who participated least? . . . Now open your eyes and share your experiences; tell each other how you felt and what you noticed about yourself and others for five or ten minutes. . . .

"Now that you have discussed your experiences and feelings of self-consciousness, I want you to become another machine. Again do this without talking or planning and with sounds, movements, and physical contact. See if you can let go more, and really enter into the activity of this machine. As you do this, be aware of how you feel and how you interact with others. Now become an automobile for about four minutes. . . .

"Now stop and close your eyes for a minute . . . and again get in touch with how you feel physically. . . . How do you feel now? . . . Absorb your experiences of the last few minutes, and become aware of how you express yourself. What part of the car did you become, what kinds of noises and movements did you make, and how did you feel as you did this? . . . How did you interact with the other parts of the car—vigorously or quietly, smoothly or with conflict, etc.? . . . How did you feel about these interactions? Who did you enjoy interacting with most and least? . . . Become aware of all the details of what went on as the group interacted. . . . Now take five or ten minutes to share your own experiences and your awareness of others. . . .

"Next I want you to become any kind of machine you want, as long as you make sounds, movements, and physical contact with others. Don't talk or plan; just start moving and making noises. If you get bored with being a part of this machine, change to being a part of a different kind of machine that you enjoy more. As you do this, continue to be aware of how you express yourself through your noises, movements, and physical contact, and how you feel and interact with the others. Now be any kind of machine you want for about six minutes. Go ahead. . . .

"Now stop, and again close your eyes and absorb this experience. Again reflect on what you experienced, and how you express yourself. . . . Now again take about five minutes to share what more you have discovered about yourself, the others in the group, and how you interact with each other . . ."

(Other machines to become: printing press, typewriter, airplane, power lawn mower, or any other machine with lots of moving parts and action. You can also do essentially the same kind of experiment by forming a group animal: octopus, elephant, dog, horse, monkey, or any animal with lots of possibilities for activity and movement.)

52   **REFERENCES**

1. Bruner, Jerome S. "On Cognitive Growth: I." In **Studies in Cognitive Growth,** edited by J. S. Bruner et al. New York: John Wiley & Sons, 1966.
2. Church, J. **Language and the Discovery of Reality**. New York: Vintage Books, 1961.
3. Clark, Frances. "Fantasy and Imagination." In **Four Psychologies Applied to Education**, edited by Thomas B. Roberts. Cambridge, Mass.: Schenkman Publishing Co., 1975.
4. Delin, P. S. "Success in Recall as a Function of Success in Implementation of Mnemonic Instruction." **Psychonomic Science** 12 (1968): 153–154.
5. Doob, L. W. "The Ubiquitous Appearance of Images." In **The Function and Nature of Imagery**, edited by P. W. Sheehan, New York: Academic Press, 1972.
6. Freyberg, Joan T. "Hold High the Cardboard Sword." **Psychology Today**, February 1975, pp. 63–65.
7. Fromm, Ericka. **The Forgotten Language: An Introduction to the Understanding of Dreams, Fairytales, and Myths**. New York: Holt, Rinehart and Winston 1951.
8. Hendricks, Gay, and Wills, Russel. **The Centering Book: Awareness Activities for Children, Parents, and Teachers**. Englewood Cliffs, N.J.: Prentice-Hall, 1975.
9. Hunter, I.M.L. **Memory**. Baltimore: Penguin Books, 1964.
10. Jung, Carl. **Man and His Symbols**. Garden City, N.Y.: Doubleday & Co. 1964.
11. Lawrence, Jodi. **Alpha Brain Waves**. New York: Avon Books, 1972.
12. Lovinger, Sophie L. "Sociodramatic Play and Language Development in Preschool Disadvantaged Children." Unpublished paper, 1973.
13. Lyon, Harold C., Jr. **Learning to Feel—Feeling to Learn**. Columbus, Ohio: Charles E. Merrill Publishing Co. 1971.

14. McKellar, P. "Imagery From the Standpoint of Introspection." In **The Function and Nature of Imagery**, edited by P. W. Sheehan. New York: Academic Press, 1972.

15. Persensky, J. J., and Senter, R. J. "The Effect of Subjects' Conforming to Mnemonic Instructions." **Journal of Psychology** 73 (1970): 15–20.

16. Piaget, Jean. **Play, Dreams, and Imitation in Childhood**. New York: Norton, 1962.

17. Pulaski, Mary Ann S. "The Rich Rewards of Make-Believe." **Today**, January 1974, pp. 68–74.

18. Singer, Jerome L. **The Child's World of Make-Believe: Experimental Studies of Imaginative Play**. New York: Academic Press, 1973.

19. Stevens, John O. **Awareness: Exploring, Experimenting, Experiencing**. Moab, Utah: Real People Press, 1971.

20. Westheimer, Benjamin. "Experiencing Education With EST." In **Four Psychologies Applied to Education**, edited by Thomas B. Roberts. Cambridge, Mass.: Schenkman Publishing Co., 1975.

The nocturnal dream is one altered state of consciousness that is common to all normal humans. In fact, recent research convincingly indicates that we cannot choose whether or not to dream [3]. Apparently, dreaming is not only biologically inherent in man but vital to mental and physical well-being. Some people vehemently deny ever dreaming, but experimental research has unquestionably refuted their denials. All people dream; they differ only in the degree to which they are able to recall their dreams.

From ancient to modern times, dreams have fascinated us and we have investigated them with varying degrees of sophistication. One of the earliest known written documents is a five thousand-year-old Egyptian book of dream interpretations [17]. Dreams have been regarded as everything from prophetic visions to cognitive excretion.

Freud theorized that dreams have two functions—to guard sleep and to periodically discharge unconscious drives [**9, pp. 39–57**]. He believed that without the dream state, the unconscious drives, permitted to surface by the lowering of regression, would lead to waking action. The other function of dreaming, discharging unconscious drives, brings the unconscious back under the control of the preconscious. According to Freud, wishes and desires that cannot be expressed consciously appear in dreams, often in a subtly disguised form. Dreams are ways in which a person can fulfill consciously unacceptable desires.

Instead of viewing dreams as a surreptitious form of wishfulfillment, Jung regarded them as subconscious representations of a given moment [**8, pp. 101–112**]. In his view, dreams do not have latent or manifest content. Jung also rejected Freud's heavy emphasis on sex in the interpretation of dreams. Adler, like Jung, viewed dreams as both purposive and causal. Both men believed that dream symbols do not have a standard meaning but have to be understood within the metamorphic context of the dream. According to Adler, dreams are spawned by the dreamer's conscious concern about unsolved problems and thus possess a future orientation.

> A dream is a bridge that connects the problem which confronts the dreamer with his goal of attainment. In this way a dream will often come true because the dreamer will be training for his part during the dream and will be thus preparing for it to come true. [**13, p. 119**]

Adler's unique concept was the notion that dreams deliberately create emotional states. He described them as "emotion factories" evoking moods that facilitate subsequent action.

In the 1950's, Aserinsky and Kleitman discovered distinct physiological cycles during sleep that are associated with dream recall [1]. Since then, the study of dreams has assumed a certain amount of scientific respectability, and dream investigations have developed a physiological as well as a psychological thrust. Numerous laboratories throughout the country are presently engaged in the electrophysiological study of sleep and dreams. Our understanding of the nature of dreaming has been greatly increased by the use of such techniques for detecting dream activity.

The average person spends one third of his or her life sleeping. Generally, sleep comes quickly and easily to the young but slowly and restlessly to the aged. Sleep is not a simple process; it occurs at a multitude of rhythmic levels during which both our minds and our bodies remain quite active. As a fundamental physiological process, dreaming is related to other rhythms of the body.

The most distinctive physiological changes during sleep are in the electroencephalogram (EEG) patterns that reveal relatively fast rhythmic waves of waking in contrast to the slower and larger wave forms of sleeping. This cyclical variation of EEG patterns occurs repeatedly throughout the night at intervals of 90 to 120 minutes from the end of one interval of rapid eye movement (REM) to the end of the next [14]. If awakened during REM intervals, subjects confirmed that they had been dreaming. Some people have as many as nine REM intervals or dreams in one night; everyone has at least three. Dreams are 10 to 30 minutes in length and tend to get longer as the night progresses. During REM, the body temperature rises and the heart rate, blood pressure, and breathing become irregular. Deprivation of REM or dream sleep has been found to increase appetite, tension, aggressiveness, and excitability [16].

Dr. Ian Oswald believes that the dream period plays an important role in brain growth and renewal, particularly in the synthesis of proteins [11].

> It has seemed to me possible that the very large amount of dream sleep somehow assists in the synthetic processes of brain repair after injury. This belief is consistent with the fact that in dream sleep, unlike slow wave sleep, the blood flow through the brain is increased far above waking levels. This suggests that it is a time of intense activity in the brain's living chemistry and to match this there is increased heat output by the brain. By contrast the blood-flow through muscles falls by two-thirds during dream sleep. [16, p. 85]

To support the theory of brain repair during dreaming, Dr. Oswald further points out that senile brain decay in the aged coincides with the fact that elderly people enjoy very little sleep in the dream state [16, p. 85].

Despite the progress made in the physiological study of dreams, our knowledge is still very incomplete. Using a film analogy, Snyder observed:

> For physiological answers to such questions as how the scripts of dreams are written, or the film produced, or why the entire process takes place, we can only wait hopefully and expectantly, but still very much in the dark. [14, p. 24].

APPLICATION OF DREAMS TO EDUCATION

Dreams are one of the major states of consciousness and therefore have a part in the development of the whole person. The formal use of dreams in an educational setting is not without precedent. An English teacher in San Francisco uses dreams as material for creative writing and drama [5]. In Connecticut, a primary teacher has children use their dreams for art projects in which the children illustrate the stories of their dreams in various media [6, p. 53].

On a more personal level, dreams can be employed as tools for self-understanding, and educational techniques have been developed to teach children to use their dreams for just such a purpose. This use of dreams is typified by Gestalt "dreamwork" in which the subject is asked to become various figures in a dream through symbolic identification. The technique of dramatizing the various parts of a dream has been shown to be a useful method in Gestalt therapy for learning to expand awareness of the personality. However, such an application of dreams is not representative of a transpersonal approach [2].

Transpersonal dreamwork is unique in that the group participates in an individual's dream experience without attempting any objective analysis. The student closes his or her eyes and recounts the dream in the present tense, as if experiencing the dream at that moment. The rest of the group close their eyes also and attempt to identify with the dreamer in order to experience the dream as completely as possible. Various degrees of participation will, of course, result. When resistance is high in a particular group member, the experience may be superficial, but this does not make it invalid. Each person is invited to share his inner life only to the degree that he is comfortable in doing so.

In a transpersonal approach to dreams, the teacher should not assume the role of a therapist who leads or interprets what is shared. Participants are allowed to proceed at their own rate; the role of the rest of the group is to offer support. In transpersonal education, sharing dream material in the classroom is designed to be a growth-enhancing experience. Its value is primarily in the area of affirmation. The process is one of learning to listen to our own and other people's dreams and allowing them to speak for themselves. The primary lesson is simply that we can learn a lot about ourselves and others by paying attention to our dreams [2].

A major source for the transpersonal implementation of dream work is found in the culture of the Senoi people who live in the Central Malay Peninsula. The Senoi consider the dream state to have a reality equal in value to that of the waking state. Their use of the dream state is so advanced that they have evolved a set of dream-working techniques that they use with one another every morning. These Senoi dream techniques, which will be described in detail later in the chapter, provide a useful model for organizing classroom dream work. One teacher describes her method as follows:

> First I found out as much as I could about the Senoi. I read the two Kilton Stewart articles and shared this information with the class. Then we discussed the Senoi and their way of life. After that I broke the class up into three "tribes" of eight children, then let them begin to share their dreams with one another with almost no help from me. The first sessions were about twenty minutes and I just floated around from one group to another. I told a few of my dreams to each group. It wasn't until after a couple of weeks that I first **did** anything like a fantasy completion or group activity. [**6, p. 92**]

Another approach to transpersonal dream work in the classroom is described by Elena Werlin in her article "Movies in the Head" [**6, p. 92**]. Closely related to Werlin's approach is one outlined by Rosemary Hayes. Her approach, despite its simplicity, proved to be "the best first experience in poetry that I have ever tried" [**5**]. Hayes describes the experience in this way:

> One day last spring I gave my Creative Writing students the assignment of bringing in the next day dreams which they had had and which they could still remember quite well. I offered no further explanation. The assignment itself intrigued them. Even as they came into the room the next day, they were all still talking about the assignment. Over the usual level of talk, I heard one student ask another, "Do you have your dream for English?"
>
> As soon as the bell rang, I gave them an assignment sheet which read simply:
>
>> Write about your dream:
>>> What does the world of your dream look like?
>>> Who is in it?
>>> What happens?
>>
>> Then if you can, think of your dream as a "vision of truth" personal or otherwise. What do you think it means?

60

Their only additional instructions were simply to be very quiet and to try to crawl back inside the dream for about five minutes to see the way it was, and to recapture the feeling the dream had given them. Then, they were to write just as fast as they could without worrying about literary style or mechanics. Their purpose was to get as much of their dream as possible down on paper in vivid, sharp, detailed language.

We turned out the lights and pulled the drapes. The room became semi-dark and very, very still.

Dreams have fascinated man since the beginning of recorded history. It is surprising that until now they have not been taken more seriously by American educators.

The past five years have revealed that a strong interest in dream research exists. The application of dreams to classroom instruction has already begun, but concrete research results are sparse. Professor M. Jouvet and his coworkers on the faculty of the College of Medicine at the University of Lyons have reported an increasing number of positive results supporting the need for dreams during sleep in order to promote healthy, conscious mental activity during the day [7]. Dr. Jouvet suggests that as part of their education, children should be taught how to use their sleep and dreams properly, since this state comprises one third of their lives.

Senoi Dream Techniques

As we mentioned earlier, the Senoi, who live in the Central Malay Peninsula, consider the dream state real. They have evolved a set of techniques for working with dreams that they use with one another every morning [6].

The late anthropologist Kilton Stewart, who introduced the Senoi dream theory to the rest of the world, summarized Senoi psychology as follows:

Man creates features or images of the outside world in his own mind as part of the adaptive process. Some of these features are in conflict with him and with each other. Once internalized, these hostile images turn man against himself and against his fellows. In dreams man has the power to see these facets of his psyche, which have been disguised in external forms, associated with his own fearful emotions, and turned against him and the internal images of other people. If the individual does not receive social aid through education and therapy, these hostile images, built up by man's normal receptiveness to the outside world, get tied together and associated with one another in a way which makes him physically, socially, and psychologically abnormal. [**15, p. 263**]

Following are several different techniques for using dreams in the classroom, arranged roughly in the order one might use them in a Senoi dream group. These techniques have been taken and/or adapted from Gay Hendricks and Russel Wills, **The Centering Book: Awareness Activities for Children, Parents, and Teachers**, ©1975, pp. 68, 71, 76–77, 79–80. They are reprinted by permission of Prentice-Hall, Inc., Englewood Cliffs, N.J.

CONTINUATION AND COMPLETION OF DREAMS. Just as we should complete unfinished business in our waking lives, we should also attempt to complete situations in our dream lives. We know that leaving matters incomplete can make our waking lives erratic and unsatisfying, and although we cannot directly see the results of unfinished business in our dreams, we can guess that it might have a similar effect. The Senoi believe that unless we complete dreams we cannot become psychologically integrated, and they have developed many techniques for the continuation and completion of dreams.

In dream work that involves continuing and completing dreams, perhaps the most frequent activity is one in which a "guide" facilitates the completion of an unfinished dream. Here are several common incomplete situations, along with suggestions for completing them.

- An object is broken—the guide helps the person put it back together.
- A person dreams of flying—the guide helps the person to go to the end of the flight, to find out who or what is there, and to bring back something of value to share with the group.
- A person dreams of climbing stairs—the guide helps her reach the top.
- A dreamer is being attacked—the guide helps him fight the attackers.
- A child falls—the guide helps him relax and continue the fall until he falls **somewhere. [6, p. 71]**

Senoi children learn at an early age to continue dreams from night to night. Though this skill may seem difficult at first, many young and old dreamers in our culture have learned it quickly [**6**]. A technique called "looping" has been found useful to help people return to previous dreams. The technique, which involves conscious repetition of certain dream images, is illustrated in the following example:

> Looping is a technique that is done just before sleep. It can be thought of as a form of suggestion, though dream images instead of verbal suggestions are repeated.
>
> This procedure can be continued during the transition from waking to sleeping, slowly looping the last part of a dream sequence in a more and more relaxed manner until one is asleep.
>
> Twelve-year-old Allen had a falling dream that he wished to complete. The teacher explains how to do it by looping:
>
> TEACHER: Maybe you could tell us what was happening during the last part of the dream?
>
> ALLEN: Mmmmm—I was sort of falling backward through the sky. It happened so fast I'm not sure.
>
> TEACHER: Can you remember enough of the feeling to get back into it tonight at bedtime?
>
> ALLEN: I think so.
>
> TEACHER: Let's try this. Tonight just before you go to sleep, let yourself get into that feeling, repeating it a few times. Over and over, feel yourself falling. As you repeat it, just relax and go with it wherever it takes you. Okay?
>
> ALLEN: Okay.
>
> TEACHER: Let us know what happens. [6, pp. 79–80]

PLANNING GROUP ACTIVITIES FROM DREAMS. One of the best ways to get in touch with dreams is to relate dream activities to group activities in the waking state. In the Senoi tribe, if the child dreams of a new trap, the elders help him to construct it to see if it will work. If he dreams a song or poem, the elders encourage him to express it for criticism and approval [15]. Similar activities can be done individually or in groups. Here are several examples of each.

GROUP

- If a child dreams of a dance or song, he is given the opportunity to lead the group in a performance.
- If a child has a dramatic dream, he is encouraged to stage a skit of the dream. He may play the role of participant or director.
- If a child dreams of a new game, he is urged to play it with the group.

- If a child dreams of a design, he is urged to draw it and then share it with the group.
- If a song is dreamed, it can be set to music to make a song. If a song is dreamed, it can be played on a classroom instrument.
- If an unusual device is dreamed, the child can be encouraged to build it, regardless of its practicality.
- If a striking image occurs, it can be the subject of a painting or drawing.
- A child can turn almost any dream into a storybook. [6, pp. 76–77]

SPECIFIC TEACHING STRATEGIES AND TECHNIQUES

There are several fascinating techniques in the use of dreams in the classroom; however, several important points must be remembered in order to incorporate dreams successfully into daily instruction.

1. Teachers must avoid interpretation. Students need the freedom to share their dream experiences, expanding and completing them as they wish, without the pressure of explanations.

2. Teachers need some experience in guiding, encouraging, and stimulating imaginative completions of dreams by students.

3. Dream work should be prefaced by a discussion with students about the significance of dreams in our lives. The practical issue of how to remember dreams should be raised. Students may be encouraged to start dream diaries.

Awareness of dreams can be expanded in several ways: by increased realization of their importance, by relating our own dreams and listening to the dreams of others, by reading the literature on dreams, and by learning and using techniques for dream recall and control.

One method for expanding dream awareness is keeping a dream journal. Students may record all their recalled dreams, even fragments, or they may restrict their entries only to clear and complete dreams. Recurring dreams should be noted with particular care, especially if they change. Students may enjoy expressing dream images in a free verse poetic form as well as in straight narrative.

ZZZ
ZZz

Dream Diary 65

To help you remember dreams, Dr. Stanley Krippner, director of the Maimonides Medical Center's Dream Laboratory, has recommended that before you go to sleep, you lie in bed and repeat aloud, "Tomorrow morning I will remember my dreams." Say it slowly at least ten times, like a chant. The rhythm of the words will help guide you off to sleep.

Keep a pad and pencil next to your bed. As soon as you wake up, write down the dream in the greatest possible detail. Relax, and try to bring back the whole dream.

If you don't remember anything, lie quietly and see what comes to you. "The first word or picture that pops into your mind is most likely related to your last dream of the night," Dr. Krippner has pointed out. "Start to free-associate on it, and it will usually take you to your dream."

When you have accumulated several weeks of notes on dreams, look through them. See what kinds of situations and which people occur most often. Notice sounds, colors, tastes, and smells that show up in your dreams. Roughly sort your dreams in any way that seems meaningful to you.

Try summing up your dreams in headlines: "Afraid to Try"; "Under Attack"; and so on. What messages are repeated? What are your dreams trying to tell you?

From **Growth Games**, p. 194, copyright © 1970, by Howard R. Lewis and Harold S. Streitfeld. Reprinted by permission of Harcourt Brace Jovanovich, Inc.

Relive a Dream

Fritz Perls suggests a method for working in depth on a single dream. "We don't interpret a dream. We bring it back to life" [**12**]. The technique is as follows:

"Relive your dream, as if it were happening now. Instead of telling the dream as if it were a story in the past, act it out in the present. Say the dream aloud, using the present tense. Be aware of what you are feeling when you say it. List all the elements of your dream: the people, animals, objects, colors, moods. Be particularly aware of any situations, such as dying, or falling, which you avoided in the dream by running away or waking up. Act out each of the elements. What does each part have to say? What do you have to say to it? What do the parts say to each other? . . . If, in your dream, there were situations you avoided, try to finish the dream by acting through the frightening situations in fantasy. Thus, if you avoided opening a door in your dream, see if you can open the door in fantasy. In so acting out the parts of your dream, you turn into a dreamer again and become one with your dreaming self. You may give words to characters whose emotions were unspoken in the dream, so that now they engage in a dialogue."

REFERENCES

1. Aserinsky, and Kleitman, N. "Two Types of Ocular Motility Occurring in Sleep." **Journal of Applied Physiology** (1955): 1–10.

2. Clark, Frances V. "Approaching Transpersonal Consciousness Through Affective Imagery in Higher Education." Doctoral dissertation, California School of Professional Psychology, No. 73-19777. Ann Arbor, Mich.: University Microfilms, 1973.

3. Diamond, E. **The Science of Dreams**. New York: McFadden Publishing, 1963.

4. Faraday, A. **Dream Power**. New York: Coward, McCann & Geoghegan, 1972.

5. Hayes, Rosemary. "Do You Have Your Dream for English?" In **Four Psychologies Applied to Education**, edited by Thomas B. Roberts. Cambridge, Mass.: Schenkman Publishing Company, 1975.

6. Hendricks, Gay, and Wills, Russel. **The Centering Book: Awareness Activities for Children, Parents, and Teachers**. Englewood Cliffs, N.J.: Prentice-Hall, 1975.

7. Jouvet, M. "The Sleeping Brain." **Science Journal** 3 (1967): 105.

8. Jung, C. **Man and His Symbols**. Garden City, N.Y.: Doubleday & Co., 1964.

9. Kramer, Milton, ed. **Dream Psychology and the New Biology of Dreaming**. Springfield, Ill.: Charles C Thomas Publishing Co., 1969.

10. Lewis, Howard R., and Streitfeld, Harold S. **Growth Games**. New York: Harcourt Brace Jovanovich, 1970.

11. Oswald, Ian. "Sleep, the Great Restorer." **New Scientist** 23 (1970): 170–172.

12. Perls, F. **Gestalt Therapy Verbatim**. Lafayette, Calif.: Real People Press, 1969.

13. Schulman, Bernard. "An Adlerian View." In **Dream Psychology and the New Biology of Dreaming**, edited by Milton Kramer. Springfield, Ill.: Charles C Thomas Publishing Co., 1969.

14. Snyder, F. **The Phenomenology of REM Dreaming**. Presented to the Association for the Psychophysiological Study of Sleep, Santa Monica, Calif., April 1967.

15. Stewart, Kilton. "Dream Theory in Malaya." In **Altered States of Consciousness**, edited by Charles Tart. New York: John Wiley & Sons, 1969.

16. Still, Henry. **Of Time, Tides and Inner Clocks**. New York: Pyramid Communications, 1972.

17. Taylor, John G. **The Shape of Minds to Come**. Baltimore: Penguin Books, 1971.

18. Ullman, Montague, and Krippner, Stanley. **Dream Telepathy**. Baltimore: Penguin Books, 1974.

19. Werlin, Elena. "Movies in the Head." In **The Centering Book: Awareness Activities for Children, Parents, and Teachers**, by Gay Hendricks and Russel Wills. Englewood Cliffs, N.J.: Prentice-Hall, 1975.

5555555 SUGGESTOLOGY-HYPNOSIS 55

Strange as it may sound, educational hypnosis can be used to free children to do their own things through greater self-discipline, self-control, and deeper learnings. The inclusion of this new technology in education would require the better training of teachers in areas of learning theory and learning processes. Educational hypnosis can potentially become a catalytic agent in changing the whole structure and strategy of education in our society.

MARTIN ASTOR

First, a brief explanation about the title of this chapter. Basically, **suggestology*** is just another word for **hypnosis**, with one important exception—the way people react to it. There is virtually no resistance to the idea of suggestology, but many people are extremely wary, if not frightened, of hypnosis. Unfortunately, hypnosis has been (and, on a reduced scale, is still being) used for entertainment purposes. The sensationalism resulting from the use of hypnosis on the stage gives it a somewhat blemished reputation, and it continues to languish in a certain disrepute despite the impressive results achieved with it in medicine, psychotherapy, and education. In order to tap its potential in these fields, an increasing number of people are using hypnosis but calling it something else, such as relaxation or suggestology. A classic example of this practice is found in **The Centering Book** by Hendricks and Wills [**9, pp. 65–68**]. They call it "the power of suggestion," but the technique is easily recognizable as an excellent example of hypnotic induction.

---

*Although the word SUGGESTION has long been used as a substitute for the word HYPNOSIS, the term SUGGESTOLOGY is a relatively new one, devised by a Bulgarian, Dr. Georgi Lozanov. It is sometimes referred to as the Lozanov Method. The Bulgarians frequently and strongly assert that it is not hypnosis, but the more they explain the theory and its use, the more apparent it becomes that suggestology is simply another term for hypnosis.

Actually, there is nothing deceptive or surreptitious in calling hypnosis suggestology or even relaxation because both of these words are descriptively accurate. Frankly, it makes more sense than trying to clean up the reputation of hypnosis. For the purpose of this book, however, it would be confusing to switch to the more recent terminology. Thus, we will continue to use the word hypnosis to identify this particular state of altered awareness.

Like dreams, hypnosis has intrigued mankind for centuries, but it continues to be a psychic phenomenon that is not fully understood.

The word hypnosis is from a Greek word meaning "sleep," an unfortunate derivation because it is much more akin to the waking state—a state, in fact, in which the subject is hyperacute rather than somnolent. Braid, the nineteenth-century Scottish surgeon who coined the term hypnosis, subsequently recognized the fallacy of equating hypnosis and sleep and tried unsuccessfully to introduce a new name.

One of the difficulties in attempting to define hypnosis is the great difference between a light state and a deep one. Consciousness is always present even in the deepest states. Hypnosis is usually defined as a state of heightened awareness with intense concentration on the suggestions presented. Suggestion itself, with or without the induction of hypnosis, can be extremely powerful. However, there is convincing evidence that indicates that an individual's receptivity and responsiveness to suggestion is significantly greater in the hypnotic state.

The history of hypnosis is popularly and professionally regarded as beginning in the eighteenth century with the rather mystical work of an Austrian doctor, Anton Mesmer. But according to Matthews, the true beginning of hypnotism dates back to 1770 in Switzerland when a former priest named Gassner discovered that he possessed healing powers and began practicing faith cures. He believed that most illnesses were caused by demonic possession. Dressed in black and carrying a crucifix, he touched the afflicted person's head and commanded the evil spirit to depart. He was credited with healing more than 10,000 sufferers [15].

Mesmer, working in Vienna, was greatly impressed with Gassner's faith healings. Mesmer believed that magnets could be used to heal and he successfully employed them with some of his patients. Later he discarded the magnets in favor of what he called "animal magnetism." He was convinced that Gassner was using some unknown force and ultimately concluded that the body possessed two poles, like a magnet, from which emanated invisible magnetic fluids. Mesmer believed that the body **was**, in fact, a magnet and was surrounded by a magnetic energy field created by the two poles of the body. Diseases were caused by the stoppage or uneven distribution of magnetic fluids, and by correcting the flow of fluids a sick person could be cured. He used passes (bodily strokes) to correct fluid imbalances. He also believed that he could magnetize inanimate objects by touching them and that once magnetized, they could be used to effect a cure. His demonstrations of animal magnetism later came to be called "mesmerism." As Mesmer's success and reputation grew, so did the jealousy and hostility of his medical colleagues. Following an investigation, he was expelled from the medical faculty and directed to either give up his private practice or leave Vienna. He went to

Paris, where the scenario was repeated. In 1784, the French Academy of Sciences denounced Mesmer's magnetism as a fraud. Mesmer retired to Versailles and later died in obscurity in Switzerland.

Despite the denunciation of Mesmer's magnetism, other medical doctors continued to investigate the phenomenon. The events connected with Mesmer's work were too compelling to be disregarded. In fact, according to Lamott, the nineteenth century was the golden age of medical hypnosis. In 1823, the first tooth was extracted under hypnosis, and three years later hypnosis was successfully used for the painless delivery of a baby [14]. In 1837, Elliotson, a British surgeon, began using mesmerism as an anesthetic and for the treatment of nervous disorders. After hearing about Elliotson's success, another British surgeon, Esdaile, used hypnosis as an anesthetic in more than 3,000 operations, of which 300 were major surgery, including 19 limb amputations. Like Mesmer, both Elliotson and Esdaile fell into disrepute with the medical profession. In fact, Esdaile was tried by the British Medical Association, found guilty, and deprived of his license.

The Scottish surgeon James Braid studied mesmerism in the middle of the nineteenth century and formulated a theory of hypnosis in his work **Neurypnology: Or the Rationale of Nervous Sleep, Considered in Relation With Animal Magnetism**. Braid's theory is noteworthy, for he treated the hypnotic phenomenon as one natural to man. His work presents hypnosis as the use of man's mental faculties in a sleeplike and suggestible mode. Later, influenced by the success of the two French doctors Charcot and Bernheim who worked with Braid's theory, Sigmund Freud tried to use hypnosis in his psychiatric practice. Unfortunately, Freud was an inept hypnotist and he gave it up in favor of free association.

The exigencies of the battlefield rekindled an interest in hypnosis during World War II. It was used to induce sleep, to treat war neuroses, to substitute for analgesics and anesthetics, and to assist the CIA. Despite these wartime discoveries, postwar usage of hypnosis was limited primarily to dentistry and obstetrics.

Although there are no statistical data, it is estimated that at the end of World War II there were no more than 200 professionals—physicians, psychologists, and dentists—using hypnosis in their practice. A conservative estimate today is 20,000. In his article "Hypnosis Comes of Age," Estabrooke states:

Today, hypnosis in practical clinical applications is expanding on all fronts. Great impetus was provided by the nod it received recently from both the British and American Medical Associations, giving it ". . . a recognized place in the treatment of certain illnesses when employed by qualified medical and dental personnel." [**6, p. 45**]

And Williams asserts that "hypnosis has recently rediscovered its place in legitimate scientific inquiry and therapy" [**19, p. 126**].

Today, a steadily increasing number of medical doctors, dentists, and clinical psychologists are using hypnosis as a therapeutic aid. Hypnosis has proved to be very useful in the treatment of stuttering, phobias, obesity, migraine, insomnia, nervous tension, intractable pain, and a wide range of psychological disorders. The black magic mystique created and perpetuated by stage hypnotism and the mass media does, indeed, show signs of disappearing, particularly in the fields of medicine and psychological counseling.

APPLICATION OF SUGGESTOLOGY-HYPNOSIS TO EDUCATION

Can hypnosis be used to improve learning? There is convincing evidence to suggest that it can be effectively applied to educational problems. In Bulgaria, Lozanov has found suggestology to be a highly efficient way to teach a foreign language. Lozanov's government-sponsored Institute of Suggestology in Sofia reportedly speeds up learning by 50 percent for both average and bright students. The instructional system, called suggestopedia, is a unique combination of suggestion-relaxation, Mauget oral methods, and traditional techniques. Teachers are individually trained both in a foreign language (French, English, German, and Italian) and in suggestion. Training in speech is also given, stressing voice patterns that are deep, well modulated, and smooth.

At San Diego State University, Cowart conducted self-hypnosis workshops to help students improve their grades. The 300 students who participated reported impressive results [**10**]. Krippner has used hypnosis to improve study skills-habits, concentration-attention, and motivation-interest and to reduce test anxiety [**12**]. Estabrooke reports a high degree of success in working with students classified as underachievers [**6**]. Illovsky is presently using hypnosis in three different schools to improve reading skills [**1**]. Jampolsky has combined hypnosis and sensory motor stimulation to help children with learning difficulties [**11**]. Krippner [**12**], Donk et al. [**3**], Mutke [**17**], and McCord [**16**] have all reported success in using hypnosis to increase reading speed and comprehension.

It must be noted, however, that the case for educational hypnosis is not completely positive. As early as 1925, Young asserted that there was no significant difference in learning or retention abilities after hypnosis [**20**]. His view was supported a decade later by Gray, who reported equivocal results in the use of hypnosis to teach spelling [**7**]. Edmonston and Stanek found that hypnosis had no significant effect on verbal learning [4], and Egan and Egan reported that hypnosis did not significantly improve academic performance [5]. Harley and Harley claimed that hypnosis actually inhibited learning [8].

At this point, the evidence supporting educational hypnosis is conflicting and inconclusive, but an extensive survey of the literature reveals that a preponderance of the evidence is positive. In 1968, Uhr, who also reviewed the research related to educational hypnosis, reported "little if any conclusive experimental evidence treating this question." But he also noted that "what evidence there is . . . indicates quite definite and possibly striking improvement in learning done while under a well-managed hypnotic trance" [18, p. 134].

It is not surprising to us that educational hypnosis is the subject of controversy, claims, and counterclaims. This is perhaps its most pervasive characteristic. For centuries, hypnosis has been shrouded in mystery; while there is an increasing trend to view and to study it more objectively, it continues to be a psychic phenomenon that is not fully understood. Even in the field of medicine, where hypnosis has gained the widest acceptance and usage, it is still a controversial technique.

To paraphrase Hilgard [10], there is strong evidence to indicate that some students benefit greatly from educational hypnosis. The hundreds of students who have improved their learning and academic achievement do not need convincing. And those who may be helped in the future should not be denied the benefit of hypnosis simply because we do not understand precisely what it is or why it works. For now, it is enough to know that, for many, it does work.

SPECIFIC TEACHING STRATEGIES AND TECHNIQUES

In a well-controlled study at Kent State University, Krippner used the following techniques in a summer remedial reading program. (In some instances, the process was called relaxation or suggestion instead of hypnosis.) During the sessions, hypnosis was employed to decrease tension while reading, to increase motivation and interest, and to increase attention span and concentration. It was also used to facilitate revisualization and reaudition of graphic symbols, thus improving spelling. At the end of the program, a statistically significant difference (.05) favoring the hypothesis was found between the experimental and control groups [13].

Following is a general hypnotic induction from Krippner that is suitable for use in a classroom. After the relaxed state is achieved, any of the suggestions/scripts given below may be used, depending on the specific educational goals.

Hypnotic Induction

"For the next few moments, let us pause and relax our bodies. We can do this at any time of the day no matter where we are. All we need to do is stop and tell our bodies what to do. First let's close our eyes and take a deep breath. PAUSE. Now concentrate on your eyelids. They are controlled by the smallest muscles in your body. Concentrate on these tiny eyelid muscles. Tell them to relax. Let your eyelid muscles become so soft, so relaxed that they seem to melt like a dish of ice cream in the sun. PAUSE. In fact they are now so relaxed that they refuse to work. Your eyes want to stay so relaxed that they refuse to open. Now relax the rest of your body. Let your face relax. PAUSE. Tell your neck to relax. Tell your chest and shoulders to relax. Tell your stomach to relax. Tell your arms and hands to relax. Tell your feet and toes to relax. Now let your mind relax. Let it become quiet and silent. Do not let any thought distract you."

The following scripts can be used with students having reading difficulties:

For Tension Problems

"Now that you are relaxed, reading will no longer be a problem for you. There is no need to worry about your reading. Start to think how much you would like to be able to read well. Imagine how good it will be to read easily and well. Relax all the muscles in your face. Feel your mouth relax. Now your eyes. You want your eye muscles to feel just this relaxed when you read. You will be able to keep your eyes relaxed and open as you read the words and lines on the page. You will see each letter in each word and read better and better."

From Stanley Krippner, "The Use of Hypnosis With Elementary and Secondary School Children in a Summer Reading Clinic," **American Journal of Clinical Hypnosis** 8 (1966): 263. Reprinted by permission of Sheldon Bradley Cohen.

hYpnosis + suggestion = imProved Reading speed + compRehension

For Motivation Problems

"Every time you read a word or a sentence correctly, you will feel very good inside. You will feel proud of yourself because you read so well. You will enjoy the feeling that reading well gives you. You will want to read some more words and sentences. You will become interested in reading books and magazines and newspapers. Every time that you read something correctly, and understand what you read, your interest will increase. You will want to read another book, or another magazine, or another newspaper. Sometimes you will make mistakes while reading. These mistakes will not bother you because we all make mistakes. None of us is perfect. However, when you read a word or a sentence very well, you will be pleased and happy. You will want to read more and more."

For Concentration Problems

"When you open your eyes, you and your clinician will select a story in a book that interests you. After looking it over for a few minutes to make certain that it is really interesting, you will start to read the story. You will find that you are able to pay very close attention to the story. You will pay close attention for many, many minutes. It will be just as if your eyes are glued to the page. In fact, you will not want to take your eyes away from the story until you have read several pages. Perhaps you will even finish the whole story. When you have trouble with a word, your clinician will help you out. But this will not affect your attention, which will be very, very strong. At the same time, your concentration will be better than it has been for a long, long time. You will think about nothing but the characters in the story and what is happening to them. You will understand what you are reading. You might even see the characters in your mind's eye. You will enjoy what you are reading. Your concentration and attention will be so good today that you will find it even easier to concentrate and to pay attention tomorrow."

From Stanley Krippner, "The Use of Hypnosis With Elementary and Secondary School Children in a Summer Reading Clinic," **American Journal of Clinical Hypnosis** 8 (1966): 264. Reprinted by permission of Sheldon Bradley Cohen.

For Spelling Problems

"Try to imagine a big, white moving picture screen. Nod your head when you have imagined the movie screen in your mind's eye (Pause). In just a moment, you will be able to imagine some big, black letters appearing on the white screen. The letters will be very clear and they will stay on the screen until the right word appears. Imagine that the letter "C" is appearing on the left-hand side of the screen. To help you imagine this, I am going to trace a "C" on your forehead. (At this point, the writer traced a "C" on the left side of the client's forehead. He traced the "C" backward so that the client would perceive it as being traced correctly.) Nod your head when the letter "C" appears on the screen (Pause). Very good. Next, imagine that the letter "A" is appearing in the middle of the screen. To help you imagine this, I am going to trace an "A" on your forehead. (At this point, the writer traced an "A" in the middle of the client's forehead.) Nod your head when the letter "A" appears (Pause). Very good. Next, imagine that the letter "R" is appearing on the right side of the screen. To help you imagine this, I am going to trace an "R" on your forehead. (At this point, the writer traced an "R" on the right side of the client's forehead. Once again, he traced it backward.) Nod your head as soon as the letter "R" appears (Pause). Very good. "C-A-R" spells "car." Can you see all three of the letters on the movie screen? Nod your head if you can (Pause). Very good. Now hold these letters in your mind's eye and concentrate on them. Make the letters a dark, dark black and make the movie screen a bright, bright white. Concentrating on the letters will help you to remember how to spell "car" when you open your eyes. Now imagine that you can hear someone saying "car." Think of what it would sound like if someone said, "car." Listen for this word in the back of your mind and you will hear it. Nod your head when you have heard it (Pause). Fine. Now keep looking at the movie screen and see how dark and black you can make

hYpnosis + suggestion = more accurate spelling

the letters. At the same time, listen for the word "car" in the back of your mind. See if you can see and hear the word at the same time. If you can, nod your head (Pause). Very good. From now on, it will be easier for you to spell the word "car." Even without thinking too much about it, you will automatically see the word "car" in your mind's eye and hear the word "car" in the back of your mind. You will soon be able to do this for other words as well. Seeing and hearing words with your eyes closed is good practice for remembering how to spell words with your eyes open. For example, you are going to open your eyes in a few minutes and you will be able to take a pencil and paper and spell the word "car."

Krippner has found educational hypnosis to be very effective in the remediation of a wide range of difficulties. A number of posthypnotic suggestions and the learning difficulties for which he found them to be effective follow.

For Problems in Study Skills and Work Habits

1.   "When you are studying this evening, you will find that your concentration is so intense that you will be interested in nothing but your mathematics assignment."

2.   "At 8:00 p.m., you will be absorbed in completing your history term paper. For the following three hours, you will want to do nothing else. Barring emergencies, nothing will interrupt you. If your friends enter the room, you will, with as much tact as necessary, send them away."

3.   "As you begin to study chemistry, your mind will quickly grasp the information at hand. Each important fact will make a profound impression upon you. You will be able to recall the information easily when future events demand it."

4.   "Before you start to study this evening, form an outline of the work you wish to accomplish so that you may, by following your outline, study very efficiently. You will accomplish a great deal as you follow this outline."

5.   "When you start working on your paper, you will organize your references and other material according to an outline of the general formation of your paper. As you plan your paper, you will become very eager to make your plan a real   nd put the ideas into writing."

From Stanley Krippner, "The Use of Hypnosis With Elementary and Secondary School Children in a Summer Reading Clinic," **American Journal of Clinical Hypnosis** 8 (1966): 264–265. Reprinted by permission of Sheldon Bradley Cohen.

From Stanley Krippner, "The Use of Hypnosis and the Improvement of Academic Achievement," **Journal of Special Education** 4 (1970): 254. Reprinted by permission of John F. Goodman, Ph.D.

For Concentration and Attention Problems

Lack of concentration or a short attention span may present a serious block to a student's academic achievement. An example of a student suffering from these problems was Robert. After studying for a few minutes, he would feel the need to open the window, get a drink of water, or visit the candy-vending machine. He would turn on the radio or record player, or remember urgent telephone calls which had to be made. Robert claimed that it had become impossible for him to concentrate on his studies for more than 10 minutes before his thoughts would wander to other matters.

Robert was hypnotized several times in a few weeks. One by one, the bad habits were replaced with other patterns of behavior. He was told that he would ignore the room temperature while he was studying; his own sensations of thirst and hunger; the appeal of the radio, the record player, and telephone. He was further told that his attention span would increase. So successful were the suggestions that, by the end of three weeks, Robert was spending several consecutive hours on his studies each night without interruption.

Lee had difficulty paying attention to classroom lectures and concentrating on the material presented. It was noticed that Lee wore a large ring; he was told that whenever his mind wandered, he merely had to rub the front of the ring to refocus his attention on the lecturer. This suggestion worked very well, and within a few weeks the new habit was so firmly established that the ring-rubbing technique no longer had to be utilized.

From Stanley Krippner, "The Use of Hypnosis and the Improvement of Academic Achievement," **Journal of Special Education** 4 (1970): 255. Reprinted by permission of John F. Goodman, Ph.D.

There is a considerable body of research documenting the causal relationship between learning difficulties and negative self-concepts. The following example of posthypnotic suggestion was effectively used by the authors to improve the self-image of a student teacher.

For Problems with Self-concept

"You are an excellent teacher. You have all the qualifications and characteristics associated with excellence in teaching. You know the subject matter well and your daily preparations are careful and thorough. You are a warm, friendly, sensitive person whom students like and respect. You are patient and have a very good sense of humor. Students trust you and find it easy to relate to you. Because of your honesty and professional dedication, other teachers and administrators hold you in very high regard.

"Visualize yourself alone in an empty classroom at the beginning of the new school year. The children have not yet arrived and you have time to enjoy the silence of the room. Focus your attention on the colors, the pale walls contrasted by the dark chalkboards; notice the sparkling desk tops and polished floors. Feel the warmth of the sun upon your arms (pause). Feel the warmth on your shoulders (pause), your neck (pause), and finally on your cheeks (pause). Let the warmth of the whole room slowly move throughout your entire body as a gentle wave in a warm lake. Let that warmth travel like a wave of peace and confidence that this school day and every school day will be peaceful and enjoyable.

"Listen to the clock and hear it click to the next minute. It is time for the students to arrive. Soon they will file in. Imagine them slowly entering one by one, and with each new face in unbroken succession let a wave of relaxation travel throughout your muscles. Now single out one particular student and follow that student through the door to some chosen desk. Imagine the enthusiasm of beginning a new year. Feel that excitement pulsate in your own body. And with that enthusiasm allow your own self to enjoy this special moment. The last student has entered and a hush fills the room as students wait in uncertainty and excitement. You are standing in the front and like a captain of a ship you can feel the smooth grain of your wooden desk under your hand, which lightly touches its surface. Your crew awaits your instructions, enthusiastically willing to launch into a fresh new year. You are ready and in full command. Past voyages and problems are dissipated like ripples in a pool. You are captain and the crew is eager to work with you.

"Since you possess all the warm traits related to highly successful teaching, you are going to find that teaching is easy and natural for you. Your self-confidence will increase with each class you teach. And as your self-confidence grows, so will your feelings of enjoyment and satisfaction. Teaching will become a source of great pride for you because you are an excellent teacher."

hYpnosis + Suggestion = more positive self concept

REFERENCES

1. Astor, Martin. "Learning Through Hypnosis." **Educational Forum** 35 (1971): 447–455.
2. Barber, T. X. "The Effects of Hypnosis on Learning and Recall: A Methodological Critique." **Journal of Clinical Psychology** 21 (1965): 19–25.
3. Donk, L. J., et al. "The Comparison of Three Suggestion Techniques for Increasing Reading Efficiency Utilizing a Counterbalanced Research Paradigm." **International Journal of Clinical and Experimental Hypnosis** 18 (1970): 125–133.
4. Edmonston, W. E., Jr., and Stanek, F. J. "The Effect of Hypnosis and Meaningfulness of Material on Verbal Learning." **American Journal of Clinical Hypnosis** 8 (1966): 257–260.
5. Egan, Richard J., and Egan, William P. "The Effect of Hypnosis on Academic Performance." **American Journal of Clinical Hypnosis** 11 (1968): 31–34.

81

6. Estabrooke, G. H. "Hypnosis Comes of Age." **Science Digest** 69 (1971): 44–50.

7. Gray, W. H. "The Effect of Hypnosis on Learning to Spell." **Journal of Educational Psychology** 25 (1934): 471–473.

8. Harley, W. F., Jr., and Harley, W. F., Sr. "The Effect of Hypnosis on Paired-Associate Learning." **Journal of Personality** 36 (1958): 331–340.

9. Hendricks, Gay, and Wills, Russel. **The Centering Book: Awareness Activities for Children, Parents, and Teachers**. Englewood Cliffs, N.J.: Prentice-Hall, 1975.

10. Hilgard, E. R. "Hypnosis Is No Mirage." **Psychology Today** 8 (1974): 120–122.

11. Jampolsky, G. G. "Use of Hypnosis and Sensory Motor Stimulation to Aid Children With Learning Problems." **Journal of Learning Disabilities** 3 (1970): 570–575.

12. Krippner, Stanley. "The Use of Hypnosis and the Improvement of Academic Achievement," **Journal of Special Education** 4 (1970): 451–460.

13. Krippner, Stanley. "The Use of Hypnosis With Elementary and Secondary School Children in a Summer Reading Clinic." **American Journal of Clinical Hypnosis** 8 (1966): 261–266.

14. Lamott, Kenneth. **Escape From Stress**. New York: G. P. Putnam & Sons, 1974.

15. Matthews, Clayton. **Hypnotism for the Millions**. Los Angeles: Sherbourne Press, 1968.

16. McCord, H. "Hypnosis as an Aid to Increasing Adult Reading Efficiency." **Journal of Developmental Reading** 6 (1962): 64–65.

17. Mutke, P. H. C. "Increased Reading Comprehension Through Hypnosis." **American Journal of Clinical Hypnosis** 9 (1967): 262–266.

18. Uhr, L. "Learning Under Hypnosis: What Do We Know? What Should We Know?" **Journal of Clinical and Experimental Hypnosis** 6 (1958): 121–135.

19. Williams, B. M. "Hypnosis Is Like a Scalpel. You Wouldn't Want It Wielded by Your Janitor." **Psychology Today** 8 (1974): 126–127.

20. Young, P. C. "An Experimental Study of Mental and Physical Functions in the Normal and Hypnotic States." **American Journal of Psychology** 36 (1925): 214–232.

6666666666MEDITATION 66

I wonder whether the yoga discipline may not be, after all, in all its phases simply a methodical way of waking up deeper levels of will power than are habitually used, and thereby increasing the individual's vital tone and energy. I have no doubt whatever that most people live, whether physically, intellectually, or morally, in a very restricted circle of their potential being. They make use of a very small portion of their possible consciousness, and of their soul's resources in general, much like a man who, out of his whole bodily organism, should get into a habit of using and moving only his little finger. . . . May the yoga practices not be, after all, methods of getting at our deeper functional levels?

WILLIAM JAMES

There is a tale cribbed from Oriental literature in which a student went to his master and asked, "How can I achieve peace of mind?" The master replied, "You can achieve peace of mind through meditation."

"And what is meditation?"

"Don't ask questions. Meditate" [**3, p. 5**].

For centuries scholars have studied meditation, and still they find it difficult to define. Paradoxically, it really doesn't matter, for in the area where meditation works, definitions lose their meaning.

During the last twelve years, thousands of people in the Western world have found that the elusive, ill-defined process known as meditation really works for them. In one large university alone, it is estimated that upwards of 2,000 students and faculty members engage in some form of meditation [**3, p. 6**]. Some take it up for spiritual development. Others try it for the feeling of exaltation or "high" that they can get from it.

There are many ways of meditating, but meditation is not the exclusive property of any particular group, religious order, or sect. It is a state of being that is independent of any faction, approach, or creed. Meditation is a frame of mind, a kind of openness to experience, a "letting go" of mental activity, which, paradoxically, may result in an increased awareness of existence. The Chinese Zen saga Bodhidharma refers to meditative discipline as "a special training outside scriptures; no dependence on words and letters; pointing directly to the soul of man; seeing into one's own nature" [**3, p. 9**]. More simply, Dr. Claudio Naranjo of the Institute of Personality Assessment and Research at the University of California states that "meditation is a dwelling upon something" [**15**]. Dr. Naranjo describes four basic approaches to meditation: the way of silence (yoga), the way of concentration (Zen), the way of surrender of self-expression (science of creative intelligence), and the way of self-awareness (biofeedback).

Daniel Goleman, who spent a year in India researching meditation for his doctorate, proposed that it was a healing force:

> I conceptualize meditation as "meta-therapy": a procedure that accomplishes the major goals of conventional therapy and yet has as its end-state a change far beyond the scope of therapies, therapists, and most personality theorists—an altered state of consciousness. [**6, p. 79**]

Goleman classifies meditation as a natural, global self-desensitization. In a state more profoundly relaxed than even deep sleep, the individual finds his or her anxieties surfacing for catharsis over a gradual period of time. Stress may be released with a recollection—more often with a twitch, shudder, or occasionally even weeping. These reactions apparently reflect resolution on an unconscious level and are fairly common to altered states.

In a sense, all meditation techniques are alike in that they all involve a focus of attention [**6, p. 69**]. The objects of concentration are numberless: a candle flame, a blank wall, a crystal mandala (a concentric geometric design), even the rising and falling abdomen. Or, with closed eyes, one can listen to a sound or phrase (a mantra) repeated mentally. One Zen method centers on an unanswerable question called a **koan**. Repetitive movements, as in the dances of the Sufi tradition, can bring about a state of trance.

An important and little-understood point discussed by psychologist Robert Ornstein is related to the preceding discussion. "However exotic the chants, contemplation, and dervish dancing may seem," Ornstein writes, the techniques "are not deliberately mysterious or exotic but are simply a matter of practical applied psychology" [**16**]. Meditation takes advantage of the structure of the nervous system to produce an altered awareness. The mystery lies not in the methods but in the brain phenomena they exploit.

84

Meditation can be approached from various vantage points; however, all the techniques share salient features. All in a sense involve a simple task of thought watching, relaxing the mind by focusing. For the sake of clarity, we will explore meditation through Dr. Naranjo's four basic approaches [15]. It must be noted that these four are not mutually exclusive nor do they necessarily cover the entire discipline of meditation. They do seem to be basic, however, and each has a uniqueness that adds to the understanding of meditation. These four approaches (the way of silence, the way of concentration, the way of surrender of self-expression, and the way of self-awareness) are presented as Dr. Naranjo has ordered them and no attempt has been made to recommend one approach as more acceptable than another. Educationally, it seems reasonable to explore all four techniques with students, thus furnishing them with alternative modes to explore further by themselves. Naturally, the available environment, materials, and time will dictate the feasibility of using these various approaches.

YOGA: THE WAY OF SILENCE

Some philosophers are of the opinion that our senses screen out a lot of information and pass along only that which is important to us in solving the problems of our daily lives. Such philosophers—among them Henri Bergson, C. M. Broad, and Aldous Huxley—believe that if we could get beyond the need to think about things, we would become aware of much of the world that is presently hidden from us. We would be able to see the true beauty of nature.

This is a modern version of a very old idea. Six hundred years ago, Indian philosophers speculated along the same line. They believed that if we could slow down the thinking processes of our minds, we could experience reality as it really is. It was from their thinking that the great meditative movement of yoga developed. In 150 B.C., the sage Patanjali stated that "yoga is the stopping of the spontaneous activities of the mind" [5]. If we follow this line of thought, we soon realize that we are dealing with a sort of give-and-take between the two major functions of our minds. The primary function is awareness, noticing the existence of something. The secondary function is thinking, trying rationally to fit a new thing into a pattern of other things we already know [3, pp. 12–13].

Yoga is a Sanskrit word that names the school of philosophical Hinduism in which it is believed that union with Brahma, the Absolute Being or World Soul, can be achieved through mental and physical discipline. Yoga offers detailed instructions for ways to suppress internal body activity, including breathing. Mental activity is also suppressed until the individual enters the state of blissful, serene contemplation of Brahma [23, p. 198].

The yoga most familiar to Westerners is hatha-yoga, or the "yoga of force," which trains the student to perform physical exercises in order to attain a state of mental and physical relaxation. Hatha-yoga is a newcomer among the many varieties of yoga that trace their origins to the teacher Patanjali. Patanjali's yoga, which he explained in his writings on the "eightfold path," became known as raja yoga, or "royal yoga." It trains the spirit rather than the body. Of the other varieties of yoga, mantra yoga—yoga that uses rhythmic sounds—has become popular because it provides the basis of transcendental meditation [2].

Westerners first became interested in yoga in the 1700s. British army surgeons in India wrote home about having seen Indians who could survive such experiences as being buried alive for a day or who could cause their hearts to stop beating. Since then, yoga has usually been accepted by Westerners grudgingly. However, since the recent

PHOTO BY LINDA GITS

investigations into altered states of consciousness, it is once again coming into the limelight. In 1973, a wire service distributed a memorable news photo of the eccentric Texas billionaire Haroldson Lafayette Hunt in a yoga **asana**, or posture. Hunt, who was eighty-three, explained, "I was reading a book that explained how yoga can add ten or twenty years to one's lifespan and decided to take it up" [**11, p. 77**].

The Menninger Institute, under the supervision of Dr. Elmer Green, has also done some well-documented research with Swami Pama, a yoga meditator, who can demonstrate remarkable control of metabolic rate and bodily functions at will. Dr. Green and his colleagues are not the only scientists currently working with yogis. Since the early 1960s, three Indian scientists, B. K. Anand, G. S. Chhina, and B. Singh, have worked with alpha activity in the meditation exercises of several yogis [**11**]. It has been shown that as these yogis entered the state of inward-turning attention called **samadhi**, the alpha waves tended to be replaced by the slower theta waves often identified with creative thinking [**11, p. 81**].

The control of breathing is a central element of the technique of yoga—more central even than the exercises and asanas [**5**]. There is a good physiological reason for the importance assigned to breathing, for our breathing is the one vital function that is controlled both involuntarily and voluntarily. Most of the time our autonomic nervous system is in charge of our breathing, which continues without any conscious control, but we can shift without effort to the voluntary motor pathway and breathe deliberately.

Prana, or the discipline of breathing, is based on the belief that there is a connection between breathing and mental states. In particular, slow and rhythmical breathing allows the practitioner to enter into mental states he or she could not otherwise reach. The ranking yoga scholar, Professor Mircea Eliade, describes the phenomenon: "Motionless, breathing rhythmically, eyes and attention fixed on a single point, the yogi experiences a passing beyond the secular modality of existence" [**5**].

The Indians were not the only people to recognize the importance of breathing in meditative practices. The Chinese Taoist philosophers Lao-tzu and Chuang-tzu were both familiar with what they called "methodical respiration," while a Chou dynasty inscription of the sixth century B.C. describes respiratory techniques. Methodical breathing found its way to Japan in the form of Zen breathing exercises. Yogic breathing has been applied to modern hypertensive therapy by Dr. Datey at the Bombay Hospital.

Through yoga, the student's field of awareness expands and there may be accompanying changes in familiar sense perceptions. Colors become intensified; objects appear to radiate light or to take on a two-dimensional appearance. If the yoga exercise is performed with the eyes closed, there may be flashes of visual imagery [**8, p. 467**]. Frequently there are changes in the ordinary perception of time: The present moment is experienced as eternity or as the stillness of absolute motion. Other physical sensations may include a feeling of warmth and changes in respiration. One emerges from the experience with a sense of physical well-being, emotional balance, and mental clarity. Interpersonal relationships seem less complicated and abrasive [**2**]. When one returns to ordinary life tasks, it is as if a hidden battery had been recharged.

Where would hatha-yoga and meditation fit into the present school curriculum? Short of squeezing new time blocks into already crowded programs, the most feasible plan would be to introduce meditation during homeroom period (that is, before first period) for grade levels seven, eight, or nine and hatha-yoga during gym period at grade levels two, three, or four [**17**].

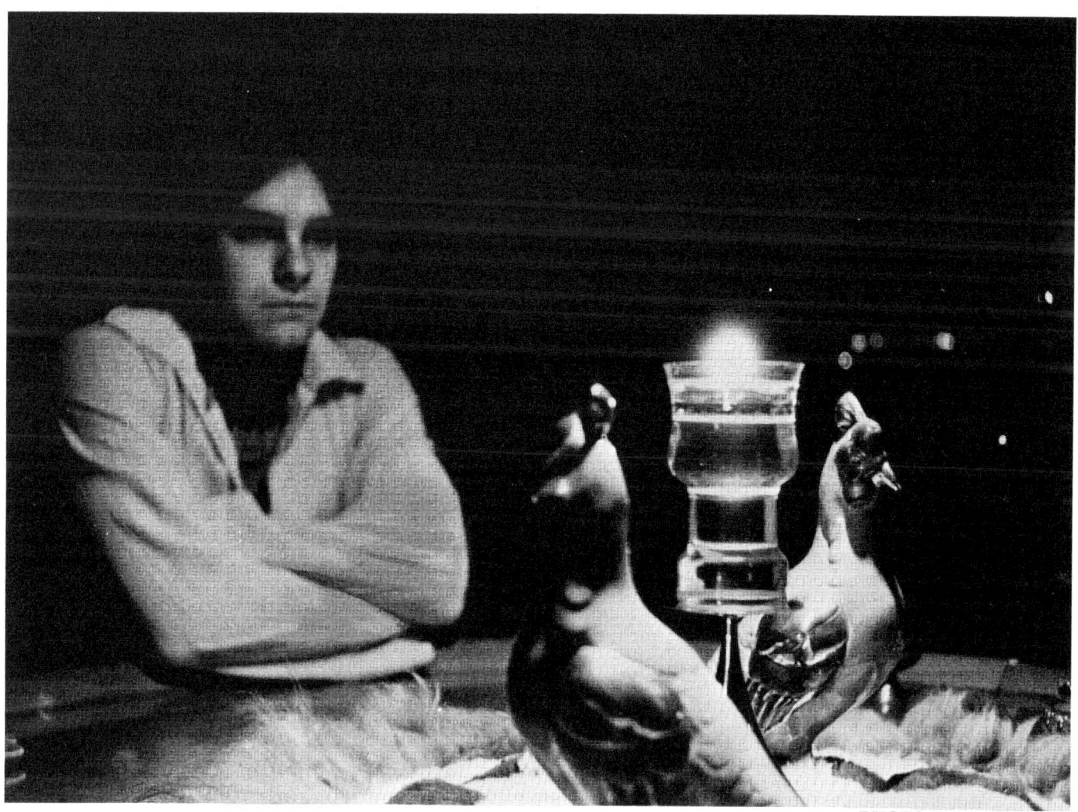

PHOTO BY LINDA GITS

88

Who would teach meditation and hatha-yoga? There are several alternatives. One possibility would be to secure the services of accomplished practitioners on a consulting basis, if per diem funds can be provided by participating schools. Another possibility would be to send interested teachers to existing training centers, if stipends can be provided for this purpose [17].

One contingency that must be anticipated is that of parental and community reaction. Along with other public relations approaches, it might be a good idea to enlist local PTA support. It will also be helpful to secure endorsements for the program from persons of established reputation in the field of education and from local administrators and officials. However, a certain amount of opposition to any new program must be expected. Hatha-yoga may be less controversial if it is incorporated into the health education program; after all, other "alien" forms of physical culture (particularly the arts of self-defense such as judo, karate, and aikido) have already been assimilated into popular culture. Meditation, however, may pose some problems insofar as it is associated with introspection. Perhaps the problem is basically a semantic one. One teacher suggested that meditation be titled "self-concept growth" [17].

ZEN: THE WAY OF CONCENTRATION

Just as yoga is often identified with bodily postures and a relaxed mental state, Zen often connotes intellectual concentration and puzzles that have a vaguely literary air. The latter characteristic was popularized by author J. D. Salinger, who used a Zen **koan**—"What is the sound of one hand clapping?"—as the epigraph of one of his books [21]. In spite of their contrasting styles, the two systems have much in common; both essentially make use of physical and mental relaxation for the purpose of increased awareness or enlightenment.

Zen is a Japanese word that means a state of absolute calmness and abstraction from the world. Like other prominent aspects of Japanese culture, it is an import, having arrived from China, where it was called **ch'an**. The Chinese, in turn, had received ch'an from India, where it was called **dhyana**, or meditation.

Although it is technically a Buddhist sect, Zen does not appear "religious" to Christian or Jewish eyes, conditioned to equating religion with belief in an omniscient and omnipotent god. Rather, Zen is a way of life whose goal is the attainment of a sense of internal peace called **satori**.

The great Zen teacher, Daisetz Teitaro Suzuki, has explained that "satori may be defined as an intuitive looking into the nature of things in contradistinction to the analytical or logical understanding of it." He goes on to say that satori is "the opening of the mind-flower," "the removing of the bar," or "the brightening up of the mind-works" [11]. Attaining satori (peace of mind, insight, and awareness of being) is accomplished by relieving the meditator of all distractions, both from the outer world and from the workings of the mind.

According to Tai-hui, a twelfth-century Zen master, the important thing "is to shut off your sense-organs and make your consciousness like a block of wood. When this block of wood suddenly starts up and makes a noise, that is the moment you feel like a lion roaming about freely with nobody disturbing him, or like an elephant that crosses a stream not minding its swift current" [11, p. 91].

The intellectual component of Zen, which has appealed to many thinkers, is, paradoxically, profoundly anti-intellectual. The style of Zen is not to reason or to argue but to know by direct intuition. Or, as the late Alan Watts once wrote, "Direct pointing . . . is the open demonstration of Zen by nonsymbolic actions or words, which usually appears to the uninitiated as having to do with the most ordinary secular affairs, or to be completely crazy"[28].

The literature of Zen is often puzzling to Westerners for it does not follow the linear reasoning process in which we have been trained. The style of these writings or puzzles is suited to the mode of the meditative mind; the writings attempt to pinpoint impressions, leaving the mind free to wander with these in order to attain insight or satori.

A typical example of a Zen sermon is presented below. It is a direct (although Westerners would probably label it oblique) sermon preached by the master Jimjo.

"As soon as one particle of dust is raised, the great earth manifests itself there in its entirety," Jimjo told the congregation. "In one lion are revealed millions of lions, and in millions of lions is revealed one lion. Thousands and thousands of them there are indeed, but know ye just one, one only." He lifted up his staff and concluded: "Here is my own staff, and where is that one lion?" [11, p. 94]

Trying to learn more about Zen, one is confronted by puzzling stories such as this and by the Four Great Statements that sum up Zen's religious content: a special transmission outside the Scriptures, no dependence on words and letters, direct pointing to the soul of man, and seeing into one's nature and the attainment of Buddhahood [29].

Considered physiologically, Zen is a means by which the body can put itself into a state of profound and strainless relaxation. Psychological changes cannot be measured as easily as physiological changes, but there is much evidence that Zen, like yoga, brings many psychological benefits [22]. Among these are not only the ability to enter an altered state of consciousness and deep relaxation but also the acquisition of a more realistic view of the world as it is and not as we imagine it to be.

The distinguished psychoanalyst, Erich Fromm, describes enlightenment as a state in which a person becomes wholly in tune with both internal and external reality: "He who awakes is open and responsive because he has given up holding onto himself as a thing, and thus has become empty and ready to receive." Fromm also says that "to be enlightened means the full awakening of the total personality to reality" [7].

Although Zen is only accidentally a system of healing, its clinical value in psychotherapy has been demonstrated in Japan. The application of Zen principles to psychotherapy seems to have developed from the success that monks had with mentally disturbed travelers who wandered into their monasteries and who were then obliged to conform to the strict rules of the refuge. A Japanese psychiatrist, Dr. Shomei Morita, has incorporated elements of Zen into a system of treatment for neurotics. The principles of Morita therapy, as it is known, are to combat egocentricity and bring the patient back into harmony with nature. The patient is encouraged to accept his or her illness in complete solitude and then, in gradual stages, is brought back into society [11].

Morita puts his patients to bed for as long as a week, forbidding them to see other patients or even their therapists. The patients are left completely alone and are not allowed to read, write, smoke, telephone, or watch television. Dr. Ilza Veith of the University of California Medical Center describes this solitary confinement: "The patient is left alone with his illness until he and his illness become one—he has to accept his illness in complete solitude" [11].

Following this rest cure, patients are encouraged to work in the hospital garden. They are reintroduced to society through contact with fellow patients, the hospital staff, and the therapist. They keep a diary, which is checked daily by the therapist, who discourages entries that harp on illness and self-importance and encourages entries that show progress toward what is considered to be a healthy reintegration into society.

As techniques of letting go, both Zen and yoga appear to be well suited to the prevention and relief of stress. They both induce profound relaxation, accompanied by physiological changes that act to relieve stress. In addition, they both have been shown to be of value in treating certain illnesses.

The use of Zen techniques in the classroom should be approached in much the same manner as the implementation of yoga techniques. Pragmatically, the basic difference in the two approaches is that the specific bodily postures that are stressed in yogic tactics are not necessary in Zen. Also, instead of mental relaxation or mind wandering, which are basic to yogic relaxation, Zen uses mental concentration as a mode of attaining insight. Consequently, in a classroom setting, the teacher uses a koan that baffles logic or a parable that points to a truth, in addition to establishing an environment of quiet in the room.

TRANSCENDENTAL MEDITATION: THE WAY OF SURRENDER OF SELF-EXPRESSION

Transcendental meditation, or TM, is the most widespread of all meditative practices in America today. Allan E. Rubatom estimates that more than 50,000 Americans have begun to practice TM within the past five years [20]. Although it is claimed that transcendental meditation is best taught by instructors of the Students' International Meditation Society, it is a very simple technique and has often been introduced in classrooms and parent groups by other instructors and teachers.

The technique of transcendental meditation is defined as:

> turning the attention inwards towards the subtler levels of a thought until the mind transcends the experience of the subtlest state of the thought and arrives at the source of the thought. This expands the conscious mind and at the same time brings it in contact with the creative intelligence that gives rise to every thought. [22]

Beneficial physiological and psychological changes allegedly result from this turning inwards. The technique itself consists primarily of mentally repeating a **mantrum**, a sound with supposedly "special" qualities, daily for a period of fifteen to twenty minutes. For reasons as yet not fully understood, this practice produces various physiological effects, including a reduction in the metabolic rate, a decline in the concentration of blood lactate, an increase in skin resistance, and an intensification of alpha activity as recorded by an EEG [27].

TM, as taught by Maharishi Mahesh Yogi, has been offered on nearly every college campus in the country through the Students' International Meditation Society. Of the approximately 50,000 Americans who have begun the practice to date, most are students and young adults. However, with the publication of scientific studies confirming TM's validity, many adults have learned the practice. TM is popular with many business and professional people, and the practice has been adopted by organizations such as Kaiser Aluminum Company and the Strategic Air Command and by scientists at the Houston Space Center, including one astronaut. The **Wall Street Journal** reported that TM has found adherents in brokerage firm partners, army generals, and a State Department expert on China who accompanied Kissinger to Peking [20].

An abundance of evidence indicates that, in addition to the relaxing changes occurring in the body, TM leads to an experience of creative energy. In fact, the purpose of TM is to help people expand their minds, develop their creative intelligence, and use their full potential in their studies, career, and recreation [30].

The first public sign that scientists had become interested in TM came in the form of a letter published in the November 1969 issue of the prestigious **New England Journal of Medicine** over the signature of Herbert Benson, M.D., of Harvard Medical School [1]. Dr. Benson described an experiment in which he had tested transcendental meditation as an alternative to drug abuse. Twenty volunteers had given up marijuana, barbiturates, LSD, amphetamines, and heroin after taking up TM. All reported that they no longer took these drugs because drug-induced feelings became extremely distasteful as compared to those experienced during the practice of transcendental meditation. Benson wrote, "Perhaps transcendental meditation should be explored prospectively by others who are primarily interested in the alleviation of drug abuse" [1].

At an international conference on drug abuse in 1971, Wallace and Benson reported on a broad study of TM as an effective answer to the problem of drug abuse [27]. Their study was based on questionnaires sent to some 2,000 meditators who had practiced TM for an average of twenty months. The results were well worth reporting. The great majority of the meditators reported that they had sharply decreased their use of drugs. Most of those who had meditated more than twenty-one months had stopped using drugs altogether. The most remarkable results were reported by the former users of hard narcotics, about 17 percent of the subjects surveyed. After twenty-one months, only 1.2 percent reported any use of narcotics at all, and all of these described themselves as light users [11, pp. 107–108].

Studies on personality development using the Personality Orientation Inventory and tests measuring determiners of happiness, indicate that subjects practicing TM do become more self-actualized, using the characteristics of self-actualized persons as summarized by Maslow: increased acceptance of self, of others, and of nature; increased ability to enjoy social interaction and to enjoy solitude; greater freshness of appreciation and emotional richness; increased autonomy and firm identity; improved interpersonal relationships; greater creativity; superior perception of reality; increased integration, wholeness, and unity of person; increased spontaneity, expressiveness, and liveliness [22].

A study by Dr. D. W. Orme-Johnson of TM's effects on autonomic stability, as measured in a test of meditators' and nonmeditators' habituation in response to a repeated stressful stimulus, found that meditators recover from stress more quickly than do nonmeditators. This indicates that meditators have more resistance to environmental stress, psychosomatic disease, and behavioral instability.

> The practice of TM, then, appears to increase the proportion of rapid habituators, indicating that meditation results in rapid recovery of homeostatic balance under auditory stress and suggesting that the physiological and behavioral attributes correlated with rapid habituation, cortical maturity, and dominance and emotional stability may also be advantages derived from the practice of Transcendental Meditation. [**19, pp. 520, 524**]

The growing acceptance and success of TM's values, coupled with its extreme simplicity, make it a technique easily introduced in the classroom. There are models for doing so already existent today, as seen in the 1974 **Phi Delta Kappan** article on Eastchester, New York public schools [4]. During 1974, Maharishi Mahesh Yogi formulated a comprehensive syllabus for the teaching of TM in junior and senior high schools. In August 1974, 130 high school teachers attended a one-month Science of Creative Intelligence Teacher Training course at Humbolt State University in Arcata, California. Nearly half of the participants received scholarships from the Department of Health, Education, and Welfare, implying a certain governmental approval. A summary of TM's potential impact is best reported in Francis Driscoll's words.

> Our experience with this program has been as successful with our adult population and faculty members as it has been with our students.
>
> As a statement of endorsement concerning the acceptance of this technique of Transcendental Meditation, this autumn of 1971, The Science of Creative Intelligence will become a regular course as part of our overall instructional program. [4]

BIOFEEDBACK: THE WAY OF SELF-AWARENESS

Although not usually directly associated with meditation, biofeedback seems to interweave all forms of such mental and physical relaxation and awareness. It is presented here as a technique closely related to yoga, Zen, and TM.

In 1958, Dr. Joe Kamiya, of the Langley Porter Neuro-Psychiatric Institute in San Francisco, found that most normal people could be trained to produce more alpha waves if they were given immediate feedback of their brain-wave patterns [25]. He accomplished this by modifying electroencephalographic equipment to produce a tone whenever a person's brain produced alpha waves. The subjects kept trying different mental gymnastics until they succeeded in maintaining a steady tone. As expected, the best way to keep the tone on seemed to be equivalent to meditating, and meditators seemed to be able to learn more quickly to keep the tone on than nonmeditators. Another biofeedback researcher, Dr. Lester G. Fehmi of the State University of New York at Stony Brook, has noted that artists, athletes, and meditators seem to show more immediate "flexible control over EEG parameters" than average subjects [12].

There is nothing new about the idea of biological feedback. At an early age, everyone learns to think and react: The thought "move hand and grab that" is followed by the hand moving to pick up the desired object. This event is both visual and muscular feedback to the central nervous system. The only new elements in biofeedback are the occurrence of instant information and the added perception that accompanies each use of the external monitoring instrument.

Biofeedback learning of self-regulation of any kind of brain wave or bodily function requires three conditions: Monitoring of the physiological activity must be continuous and sensitive enough to spot instant-to-instant alterations, physiological facts must be given back quickly, and one must want to learn how to do it. Biofeedback uses many tools—EEG to measure brain wave, EKG (electrocardiogram) to graph heart processes, GSR (galvanic skin response) to measure skin response, and EMG (electromyograph) to check muscle tension. Most of the original research, however, deals with EEG reports on the brain and EMG records of the relaxation of muscle tension.

Using this machinery, biofeedback acts as a mirror for things we cannot see with the naked eye, opening a universe for exploration. A toothache is a feedback that cannot be seen. The ache is invisible, but it exists and sends sensory stimuli to the brain, resulting in a real feeling of pain. Other feedbacks we take for granted are falling asleep when tired, sweating when hot, eating and digesting food when hungry, or hitting a golf ball with a golf club. Biofeedback merely takes on more signals of a physiological function and converts the information in that external feedback device to let us perceive this internal fact in our external perceptual world. And this is when "it" happens. As we perceive it, we get the "feel" of it and have a chance to control it. Consciously, we may not know how we do it, but we can "feel" how to do it. Such control can be as sophisticated as the willful firing of just one or two of the millions of muscle nerve units, a feedback phenomenon already demonstrated in studies by Dr. John Basmajian [12].

Some efforts have been made toward introducing biofeedback exercises in the classroom [26], but pragmatic problems related to the purchase of feedback devices make such implementation difficult. Nonetheless, biofeedback has been shown to be closely related to meditative states and has the potential of increasing self-awareness and control.

APPLICATION OF MEDITATION TO EDUCATION

Writing about teaching styles in the affective education movement, Douglas H. Heath, professor of psychology at Haverford College and a researcher on student development, described a new type of education that he believed should be fostered in students.

> My understanding of man tells me the deepest source of the creative-aesthetic impulse is in our less conscious and more primitive inner world, and that we make contact with it through a receptive meditative attitude. Not until we learn how to reach and touch and then channel and witness our inner voices will we be truly educable. If a youth learns how to develop such accessibility to his inner powers and integrates such forces and insights with more social modes of communication, then I have no fear for him. He will have developed a capacity for resiliency and autonomy that will enable him to cure his estrangements and create his own adaptations to his unknown society of the future. He will come into control of his growth. . . . Within a few years, schools and colleges will be offering courses on meditation. Fanciful? Not at all. One of the exciting frontiers of psychological research is the demonstration that man can secure much greater access to and control over his consciousness through meditation than most of us have thought possible. [9]

Heath's prescription for the integration of creative intelligence in each individual student through meditation is no longer merely a theoretical suggestion. Within the past five years, a growing number of educators have been incorporating meditative techniques into classroom experiences. Admittedly, yoga and Zen have been received less enthusiastically than Transcendental Meditation, and biofeedback approaches are usually relegated to college campuses because of the need for electronic feedback devices. Nonetheless, all four approaches, especially TM, are being used in classrooms with many positive results.

One noteworthy systematic approach using meditation in the classroom is represented in the Eastchester public schools of New York [4]. Employing the services of the New York Students' International Meditation Society, the school system systematically introduced meditation to the students. An introductory lecture was presented to all students in the senior high school and four trained meditators were available to individual students throughout the day on a one-to-one basis. Not only was the student response favorable but in a relatively short period of time, 12 percent of the faculty were participating in the meditation program. In February 1971, meditation was introduced into the local adult education program. Perhaps the most striking proof of the success of these programs is that the meditative techniques are still being offered in the schools. In evaluating the impact, Francis Driscoll reports:

> Reflecting upon our modest success, we feel that it is attributable to the great potential for student welfare that the practice of transcendental meditation offers. Another vital factor in the success of our program was the well-thought-out, comprehensive community and parent information program carried out in the autumn and early winter of 1971 before we introduced TM to the student population.
>
> Finally, we believe that transcendental meditation has been of direct and positive help to students in our secondary school who have begun to meditate. Students, parents, and teachers report similar findings. Scholastic grades improve, relationships with family, teachers, and peers are better, and, very significantly, drug abuse disappears or does not begin. [4]

Intense sensory awareness has been shown to be related to meditation. Graham found that twenty minutes of meditation lowered the auditory thresholds for discrimination of frequency and amplitude. Intense color perception is often said to follow meditation, as well as synesthesia, a peculiar blending of senses that may result from atypical neural activity. This phenomenon is not uncommon in altered states. In his **Autobiography of a Yogi**, Paramahansa Yogananda recalled that his guru had promised that "the eyes shall hear, the ears shall see" [**6, p. 76**].

Meditation has been shown to be related to certain peak experiences, seemingly egoless awarenesses that are beyond time and space, good and evil. They involve a giving up of the self to receive inspiration and knowledge. Maslow notes that they are intense identity experiences in which the creator becomes one with the work being created in the same way as a mother may feel one with her child. Attainment of integration, identity, and autonomy of selfhood is simultaneously a transcending of the ordinary sense of self. These experiences seem to result from certain "triggers" [**19, p. 442**].

The triggers that set off transcendent ecstasy can include natural scenery, sexual love, childbirth, movement, religion, art, scientific or poetic knowledge, creative work, introspection, or beauty. In addition to these natural triggers, meditation seems to offer another possibility. In a recent study, Marghanita Laski refers to the use of the meditative discipline [**14**]. Defining meditation as a mental exercise in which attention is focused on an object, image, or bodily process, Laski suggests that the student may be trained to watch, rather than direct, his or her thoughts or to concentrate on an intellectually unsolvable paradox, as in the training of Rinzai Zen. Through this activity, the student's attention bypasses ordinary cognitive functioning. The meditator first becomes a passive witness of his or her own consciousness, then identifies with and becomes his or her true self, the source of consciousness.

Driscoll reports that his students found that meditation improved their grades and their social relationships and decreased their use of drugs [**4**]. The last is especially interesting in light of Weil's contention that people have a natural desire to experience altered states of consciousness. If we assume that Weil is correct, then meditation and other forms of altered consciousness might be useful substitutes for drugs. A transpersonal drug education program could teach people how to control and explore their consciousness in nondrug ways [**19, p. 339**].

Behavior is also favorably affected by meditation. Psychological tests given at the University of Cincinnati seem to show that meditators, as a group, are happier than nonmeditators. A "self-actualization" test was designed to show to what degree an individual was using his or her full potential [**18**]. Thirty-five students participated in the study. Fifteen were then taught how to meditate and, two months later, all were retested. The meditators scored significantly higher on six of twelve indexes of self-actualization. The other students remained at about the same level [**18, p. 19**].

Some other results of meditation include:
1. increased energy and efficiency in performing work
2. increased calmness, decreased physical and mental tension

3. increased creativity, productivity, inventiveness, discrimination, intuitiveness, and concentration

4. loss of desire for or complete elimination of hallucinogenic or depressant drugs such as LSD, marijuana, amphetamines, tobacco, coffee, or alcohol

5. attenuation of bad body posture, insomnia, and high blood pressure

6. better mobilization of body resources to combat various strenuous circumstances such as accidents, sensory monotony, physical confinement, injury, etc. [18]

SPECIFIC TEACHING STRATEGIES AND TECHNIQUES

A Basic Meditation Technique

Four basic elements are common to all forms of meditation:

1. a peaceful environment
2. a mental pivot point
3. a silent, receptive attitude
4. a comfortable position [1]

The following exercise incorporates these four elements in a simple, direct experience and does not attempt to employ any specific meditative approach.

1. The teacher should establish quiet, calm surroundings, eliminating as many distractions as possible. Background sounds should be kept to a minimum. If a classroom is used, a PLEASE DO NOT DISTURB sign should be hung on the closed door.

2. The students should choose or be given a one-syllable sound or word to be repeated silently and slowly during the period of meditation. Traditionally, words containing a resonant M or N have proven most successful; hence, the Sanskrit "ohm" or the English "one" are good choices. The purpose of the repetition is to free the meditator from logical, externally stimulated thought by focusing the mind on an activity that requires no mental activity other than concentration.

3. Students should be instructed not to be concerned about how they "should" feel or about what "ought" to happen. The only goal is relaxed concentration on the chosen word. When distracting thoughts enter the mind, they should simply be disregarded and the mind should be refocused on the sound repetition.

4. Students should assume comfortable positions, either at their desks or perhaps on the floor. Clothing should not bind, and muscular effort should be minimal.

Using these four basic elements, one can achieve relaxation. Students may be instructed as follows:

"In peaceful, quiet surroundings, find a comfortable position.

"Close your eyes.

"Speak to all your muscles, telling them, one by one, to release all tension, to relax completely. Begin with your feet and move slowly to your head. Speak to your toes, ankles, calves, knees, thighs, lower torso, spine, upper torso, shoulders, neck, head, face—until your entire body is entirely relaxed and tension-free. Feel your body become pleasantly heavy; let it sink gently into the floor or chair.

"Close your mouth so that you breathe only through your nose. Focus your attention on your breathing. Each time you breathe out, say your special word silently to yourself. Match your breathing to the relaxed, rhythmical repetition of your word.

"We will continue this exercise for five minutes. I will tell you when to stop."

(After five minutes—the time can be slowly lengthened to twenty minutes as the group becomes accustomed to meditation): "Our meditation time for today is over. Keep your eyes closed for a moment as you reorient yourself to resuming ordinary activity. Now open your eyes."

Yoga Meditation Techniques

There appears to be no reason why yoga meditation techniques should not be incorporated in the elementary grades. Some educators claim, however, that because of the somewhat oblique approaches employed in the practice of yoga, it is a technique best postponed until adolescence [**19, pp. 450–500**].

During adolescence, physiological changes contribute to the child's altered self-perception and life goals are becoming important. Meditation should be introduced into the curriculum at the seventh or eighth grade level. Whether or not it will be effective at this level is an empirical question to be determined by the results of the program. Although we know that average college students are receptive to meditation, in the case of younger children we are simply making educated guesses on the basis of limited observations.

One type of yoga meditation is that of focusing on a "seed." The seed may be a simple object or thought. Before introducing this exercise, the students should be relaxed and in a quiet environment.

"For one minute look at the second hand of your watch, without losing your visual focus or mental attention. This practice in emptying your mind to increase sensitivity is almost impossible to do the first few tries. Your mind will seem not under your control. Only after you've had practice will you be able to avoid thinking about other things.

"Here is another experiment in meditation on an object. Concentrate on your hand. Observe the lines, the color, the texture, the shape in space, the shapes of the mounts and bases. Feel the warmth within the hand and the sensation of air around it.

"Meditate on your hand so that it fills your entire consciousness. You are likely to arrive at a sensation of being in two places at once: at one with your hand, since you will be exquisitely sensitive to it, yet unconnected to it, observing it detachedly from a distance.

"Concentrate on an object that pleases you—a piece of sculpture, a vase, a flower. If you're concentrating on a flower, try to see the total flower as it exists in itself—devoid of all associations, labels, connections with other things and places and times. Exclude from the meditation your ideas and experiences concerning flowers, and avoid analyzing the flower, separating it into its parts or however else you may treat it intellectually. Keep the object of your meditation pure. Concentrate on it alone. Let your perception of it fill your mind."

The following steps are an outline of how to reach a deeply relaxed, meditative stage.

1. POSITION.   "Find a very comfortable chair where you can be by yourself in a quiet room with just soft light. Not dark. Make sure that the chair fits you where you can relax all the muscles in your body. The position you take is very important in relaxation and meditation. You should be able to let go and relax in it, yet not fall asleep. Move around in the chair until all your body is comfortable and resting. The yoga positions (such as the cross-legged lotus positions) or other meditation postures are not necessary for most persons. A straight-backed chair can be used with feet planted wide apart and flat on the floor. The most comfortable height should be adjusted with cushions. A less erect posture in an ordinary easy chair can also be used."

2. DISTRACTIONS. "How to handle distractions is important. The aim of this relaxation technique is increasing awareness of what is happening inside. At first, concentrate only on finding a comfortable position and making sure you stay comfortable and relaxed. Do not think of anything, but do not prevent thoughts. If there are distractions from outside, simply let them pass. You will discover after a few relaxation sessions that the more you practice, the less outside distractions will bother you."

3. BREATHING. "How you breathe is extremely important. Close your eyes and concentrate on slowing down breathing to a regular deep rate on inhale, then exhale. Let your breathing become relaxed and free-flowing, so that the movement is mainly in the abdomen. Do not force air in. Let it come to you slowly. Exhale freely, getting all the air out of your lungs. Listen to the breathing and concentrate just on that. Practicing this breathing exercise for a while will already shift your awareness into a very relaxed thought-free state. Don't block it. Let it happen."

4. THE FACIAL MUSCLES. "Concentrate on your face and relax your jaw muscles. This is difficult for many persons. If you find it difficult, clench your teeth and tense your jaw muscles once or twice and then let them relax. Let your mouth hang slightly open, the jaw slack. Then concentrate on relaxing your forehead muscles (the frontalis muscle). The frontalis is one of the more important muscles in the body to relax. It may be difficult at first, but again, if you have trouble with it, tense it first and then let it relax. Many persons have difficulty with the facial muscle step, and must practice relaxing the facial muscles before moving to the next step."

Note: "Don't push it!!! Some persons will not be able to go through all the steps in one session. These steps are designed for relaxation, meditation, and perception, not tension. If you feel exhaustion rather than relaxation, stop. . . . Try again later or on the following day. Keep going as long as you remain relaxed. If you become tense, stop!!!"

---

5. THE CIRCLE. "Relaxation of the facial muscles begins the actual "circle." Concentrate on relaxing the right ear, then the right hand, then the right foot, one after the other, as relaxation occurs. Then around the circle to the left ear, and back to the face. Concentrate on these parts of the body one at a time, until you can feel them absolutely relaxed and you have complete control over them. For some persons, this circle technique works better when they go around the circle in the opposite direction, such as face to left ear, then left hand, and left foot. Then to the right foot, right hand, and right ear to face. Try both to see which is best for you."

6. ALPHA STATE. "When breathing and the magic circle of relaxation have combined, all thoughts and thinking should be stopped, as if preparing to go to sleep. (Don't go to sleep!) By now you should be in the alpha state of relaxed awareness. At this point, there should be very little thought and only detached observation is maintained."

7. THETA STATE. "Next, if it is not disturbing, partially open your eyes (just enough to let some dim light in), and let your favorite daydream occur. This daydream may be a fantasy. Some persons use a very pleasant memory, and "let go" and allow the pleasant memory to run freely without control. The theta state of self occurs when there is imagery such as that produced in a daydream, fantasy, or pleasant memory. It is in this state that psychic imagery is usually experienced."

8. CREATIVITY. "By now you should have cast off all roles and behavior of everyday life. If you can learn to control at will this theta state of consciousness, you will be able to be creative at will. For example, musicians will get into such a state and actually experience a full orchestra playing a musical composition which the musician is at the same time creating. Artists will create a new painting. Mathematicians will create new formulas. Persons can develop new psychic experiences with ease."

From J. S. Martindale, "The Magic Circle." Reprinted by permission of J. S. Martindale.

A Zen Meditation Technique

It is often difficult to distinguish one meditative approach from another because all forms of meditation are related. However, each has a certain accent or highlight. Concentration techniques are considered to be representative of the use of Zen.

Zen, by its very nature and goals, seeks to develop the will and powers of concentration, so it is particularly applicable and relevant to education. Becoming one with the object of meditation provides an actual experience of transpersonal consciousness. When subject and object merge, even momentarily, the experience is both transcendent and self-validating. Such an effect of meditation is certainly not automatic; it requires persistent, consistent practice. However, even a limited introduction to Zen in the classroom may inspire students to pursue the practice on their own.

Initially, concentration meditation is facilitated by focusing on an external object. A candle flame, a pinpoint of light on a screen, a mandala, or a mantra are suitable objects for visual meditation. Concentration may also be aided by auditory stimuli, such as repetition of a mantra, or a tape loop with a single repeating word, such as "cogitate."

Concentration meditation may also be practiced with eyes closed, in which case emphasis is on the development of inner vision. A simple introductory exercise is one in which participants are asked to visualize a white dot inside a white circle on a black background for four minutes, then a white plus sign on a black background for four minutes, and then a white triangle on a black background for four minutes. Initial attempts are usually discouraging. Participants are likely to be surprised by how little control they have over their imagery and how difficult the exercise is. It is useful in demonstrating the ineffectiveness of the will and is used in psychosynthesis as an exercise for the development of will. Students may be encouraged to experiment with the effects of daily practice over a period of several months.

Other forms of concentration meditation which do not involve external aids include concentration on a word, on an idea, on a color, on a scene from nature, or any appropriate symbol. One excellent introductory meditative exercise involves simple concentration on breathing. The student may be instructed to simply observe each breath, or he may be instructed to count his breaths from one to ten and then start again, and continue the process of counting breaths from one to ten for a period of ten to twenty minutes. Initially, a short period of meditation such as ten minutes, may seem long, but as practice continues, the period of time may be lengthened to forty-five minutes, according to what is appropriate to the situation.

From Frances V. Clark, "Approaching Transpersonal Consciousness Through Affective Imagery in Higher Education." Doctoral dissertation, California School of Professional Psychology, 1973, No. 73-19777 (Ann Arbor, Mich.: University Microfilms). Reprinted by permission of Frances V. Clark.

Transcendental Meditation Techniques

TM is by far the most popular meditative technique being used in classrooms in the United States. One can study the technique formally through the International Meditation Society, headquartered in Los Angeles. However, it is not hard to learn meditation rooted in TM principles without a teacher.

First, find a quiet place where you won't be disturbed. (Later, you will find that you can meditate anywhere.) At the beginning, however, the main thing is to be sure that you aren't going to be interrupted. It's hard not to feel self-conscious and nervous if there's a chance that somebody may blunder in and demand to know what you're doing.

Choose a mantra. Either OM, which is considered to be the supreme mystic syllable, or SHOM, which is also known to have considerable power, is appropriate. Other potent mantras are said to be AYN, HUM, and MU.

Most mantras have an interesting common feature. Almost without exception they include M or N (and frequently H), sounds which seem to resonate through the head even when repeated silently. A survey of liturgical chants of churches, the sonorous incantations of primitive tribes, and the Sanskrit mantras suggests that mankind has an ancient, intuitive knowledge of the most powerful methods of altering consciousness through auditory stimuli.

Posture is not particularly important so long as you are comfortable. The lotus posture is for other people. Sitting upright is perfectly acceptable and is in fact a yoga posture called the maitreya asana. Don't slump. Keep your back and neck upright.

Take two or three breaths, close your eyes, and begin to say the mantra over and over. Thoughts will spring to the surface of your mind. Whenever they do, go back to the mantra. That is all there is to it. Continue for twenty minutes or so, and in any case for not less than fifteen minutes. When you are through, open your eyes, breathe deeply, and stretch.

Don't be discouraged by the impression that nothing is happening. That is precisely the point: on the level of conscious thought, nothing is happening.

While nothing is happening in your mind, something measurable may be going on in your body. Take your heart rate, breathing rate, and finger temperature after meditating. Record them day by day on the charts. When your pulse and breathing slow down and your hands become warmer after meditating, you are well on the way. You have learned how to let go.

From Kenneth Lamott, **Escape From Stress** (New York: G. P. Putnam's Sons, 1974), pp. 114–116. Reprinted by permission of G. P. Putnam's Sons and McIntosh, McKee & Dodds, Inc.

Movement Meditation

"Yet another form of meditating to sound is to move with music. Lie on the floor, and immerse yourself in a musical composition. Play it over and over again, and follow individual instruments, the rhythm, the melody. Let the body move as it will. Even if 'unmusical,' you're likely to transcend a merely auditory experience and feel the music throughout your body. Try listening not only with your ears, but with all parts of your body—your armpits, fingertips, . . . and toes.

"Follow through on the first movement that comes to you. Make it wider, larger, stronger, softer. Let more and more of your body move. Your hands, shoulders, legs, have something to express—let them speak."

From **Growth Games**, p. 71, copyright © 1970 by Howard R. Lewis and Harold S. Streitfeld. Reprinted by permission of Harcourt Brace Jovanovich, Inc.

The following is a simple movement meditation that can be done indoors and outdoors. It is a good activity for turning down the volume of our mental chatter while becoming more aware of our experience of the world around us.

"Much of the time we are not aware of how we move through the world, because we are too busy listening to the chatter in our minds. Today, as we walk we will do something to quiet our minds while we walk, so we can be more aware of how we move and how we make contact with the earth.

"And now let's begin walking along, smoothly and easily, and as we find a pace that feels good, not too fast and not too slow, let's begin to say this sentence in time with our walking. The sentence is "I listen and I see." And now let's all begin saying it out loud.

(Pause: twenty seconds)

"Now, as we move, let's say the sentence quietly to ourselves.

(Pause: twenty seconds)

"And now begin saying the sentence in your mind, smoothly and easily. If your mind wanders, simply return to saying, 'I listen and I see.'

(Walk for three to five minutes)

"And now let's slow down and stop. Let's close our eyes and stand still for a moment . . . feeling calm and peaceful . . . feeling our feet and how they make contact with the earth. And when you're ready open your eyes, letting a feeling of rested alertness fill your bodies."

From Gay Hendricks and Russel Wills, **The Centering Book: Awareness Activities for Children, Parents, and Teachers,** ©1975, pp. 33–34. Reprinted by permission of Prentice-Hall, Englewood Cliffs, N.J.

AN EPILOGUE

Research on altered states of awareness is still in its infancy. The full impact of transpersonal education will not be felt for decades; however, it already seems evident that the transpersonal phenomenon is a threshold development, one leading to vistas and realities never experienced by man. Perhaps the development of these altered states of awareness may lead to that fourth or fifth dimension to which philosophers and scientists alike address themselves. Perhaps transpersonalism is the road that leads the old to dream dreams, the young to see visions, and all to witness miracles once again.

REFERENCES

1. Benson, Herbert. "Your Innate Asset for Combating Stress." **Harvard Business Review** (1974): 49–60.
2. Clark, Frances. "Fantasy and Imagination." In **Four Psychologies Applied to Education**, edited by Thomas B. Roberts. New York: John Wiley & Sons, 1975.
3. Costain, Edward E. **Meditation for Peace of Mind**. New York: Dell Publishing Co., 1975.
4. Driscoll, Francis. "TM as a Secondary School Subject." **Phi Delta Kappan** 54 (1974): 236–237.
5. Eliade, Mircea. **Yoga: Immortality and Freedom**, 2nd ed. Translated by Willard R. Trask. Princeton, N.J.: Bollingen Series LVI, 1969.
6. Ferguson, Marilyn. **The Brain Revolution**. New York: Taplinger Publishing Co., 1973.
7. Fromm, Erich. **The Art of Loving**. New York: McGraw-Hill, 1968.
8. Green, Elmer E., and Green, Alyce M. "The Ins and Outs of Mind-Body Energy." In Science Year, **The World Book of Science Annual**. Chicago: Field Enterprises Educational Corp. 1973.
9. Heath, Douglas. "Affective Education: Aesthetics and Discipline." **School Review** 80 (1972): 353–372.
10. James, William. "Writings." In **Psychical Research**, edited by G. Murphy and R. V. Ballou. New York: Viking Press, 1963.
11. Lamott, Kenneth. **Escape From Stress**. New York: G. P. Putnam's Sons, 1974.
12. Lawrence, Jodi. **Alpha Brain Waves**. New York: Nash Publishing Co., 1974.
13. Lewis, Howard, and Streitfeld, Harold. **Growth Games**. New York: Harcourt Brace Jovanovich, 1970.
14. Murphy, Michael. "Education for Transcendence." **Journal of Transpersonal Psychology** 1 (1969): 21–32.
15. Naranjo, Claudio, and Ornstein, Robert E. **On the Psychology of Meditation**. New York: Viking Press, 1971.
16. Ornstein, Robert. **On the Psychology of Meditation**. New York: Viking Press, 1971.
17. Richard, Michael. "Attention Training: A Pilot Program in the Development of Autonomic Controls." **Contemporary Education** 43 (1972): 57–60.
18. Robbins, Jhan, and Fisher, David. **Tranquility Without Pills**. New York: Bantam Books, 1972.
19. Roberts, Thomas B., ed. **Four Psychologies Applied to Education**. New York: John Wiley & Sons, 1975.
20. Rubatom, an E. "Transcendental Meditation and Its Potential Uses for Schools." **Social Education** 12 (1972): 851–857.

108

21. Salinger, J. D. **Catcher in the Rye**. New York: McGraw-Hill, 1969.
22. Seeman, William; Nidich, Sanford; and Banta, Thomas. "Influence of Transcendental Meditation on a Measure of Self-actualization." **Journal of Counseling Psychology** 19 (1972): 184–187.
23. Still, Henry, **Of Time, Tides, and Inner Clocks**. New York: Pyramid, 1975.
24. Tart, Charles, ed. **Altered States of Consciousness**. New York: John Wiley & Sons, 1969.
25. Timmons, B., and Kamiya, J. "The Psychology and Physiology of Meditation and Related Phenomena: A Bibliography." **Journal of Transpersonal Psychology** (1970): 41–59.
26. Toomin, M. K., and Toomin, H. "Biofeedback: Fact and Fantasy! Does it Hold Implications for Gifted Education?" **Gifted Child Quarterly**, Spring 1973, pp. 48–55.
27. Wallace, R. K., and Benson, H. "The Physiology of Meditation." **Scientific American** 226 (1972): 84–90.
28. Watts, Alan. **The Way of Zen**. New York: Pantheon Press, 1957.
29. White, John, ed. **The Highest State of Consciousness**. Garden City, N.Y.: Anchor Books, 1972.
30. Yogi, Maharishi Mahesh. **Transcendental Meditation: Serenity Without Drugs**, formerly titled **The Science of Being and Art of Living**. New York: Signet Press, 1963.

AUTHORS

Alton Harrison, Jr., Ph.D., Professor
Diann Musial, Ed.D., Instructor
DEPARTMENT OF SECONDARY AND ADULT EDUCATION
NORTHERN ILLINOIS UNIVERSITY
DEKALB, ILLINOIS 60115

RECENT PUBLICATIONS

"Ideal Child and Successful Student—Are They the Same?" **Phi Delta Kappan**, May 1974, pp. 635-636.

"Educational Reform— A Balanced Perspective." **The Educational Forum**, March 1974, pp. 331-336.

"Traditional vs. Emergent—A Study of Value Change." **The Intellect**, March 1974, pp. 398-400.

"An Assessment of Teacher Influence." **The Clearing House**, December 1973, pp. 227-231.

"Teacher Accountability—A Fallacious Premise." **Kappa Delta Pi Record**, February 1973, pp. 75-76.

"A Plea for Research Subjectivity." **Improving College and University Teaching**, Winter 1973, pp. 38-39.

"Educational Controversy—A Gloomy Prediction." **Contemporary Education**, November 1972, pp. 115-117.

"Educational Reform—Where Will It Lead Us?" **The Educational Forum**, May 1972, pp. 542-543.

"Individual Instruction—A Word of Caution." **Kappa Delta Pi Record**, April 1972, pp. 105-106.

"Student Views of Higher Education." **University College Quarterly**, January 1972, pp. 15-20.

INDEX